1001
THINGS TO DO
IF YOU
DARE

ben malisow

ADAMS MEDIA
AVON, MASSACHUSETTS

For the redhead, who made it happen. I love you.

Published by Adams Media, an F+W Publications Company
57 Littlefield Street, Avon, MA 02322 U.S.A.
www.adamsmedia.com

ISBN 10: 1-59869-120-1
ISBN 13: 978-1-59869-120-7

Printed in the United States of America.

J I H G F E D C B A

Library of Congress Cataloging-in-Publication Data
Malisow, Ben.
1001 things to do if you dare / Ben Malisow
p.   cm.
ISBN-13: 978-1-59869-120-7
ISBN-10: 1-59869-120-1
1. Conduct of life—Humor. 2. Adventure and adventurers—Humor. I. Title. II. Title: One thousand and one things to do if you dare. III. Title: One thousand one things to do if you dare.
PN6231.C6142M35 2007
818'.602—dc22
2006036471

Due to the potential for hazard, every precaution should be taken before attempting any actions listed in this book. The author, Adams Media, and F+W Publications, Inc. do not accept liability for any injury, loss, or incidental or consequential damage incurred by reliance on the information or advice provided in this book.

This publication is designed to provide accurate and authoritative information with regard to the subject matter covered. It is sold with the understanding that the publisher is not engaged in rendering legal, accounting, or other professional advice. If legal advice or other expert assistance is required, the services of a competent professional person should be sought.
    —From a *Declaration of Principles* jointly adopted by a Committee of the American Bar Association and a Committee of Publishers and Associations

Many of the designations used by manufacturers and sellers to distinguish their products are claimed as trademarks. Where those designations appear in this book and Adams Media was aware of a trademark claim, the designations have been printed with initial capital letters.

Interior illustrations: background grunge texture ©iStockphoto.com/maigi, footprints ©iStockphoto.com/appleuzr, cigarette burn ©iStockphoto.com/michael1959, coffee mug ring ©iStockphoto.com/ranplett.

This book is available at quantity discounts for bulk purchases.
For information, please call 1-800-289-0963.

CONTENTS

FOREWORD

Wow. Here I was thinking I had experienced the biggest thrills of life, and then this manuscript ends up in front of me. Ben has gone to great depths to investigate all of the fear-inducing activities this planet has to offer. I am blown away by some of the random ideas in there that only a true thrill-nut would think up. I have made my own lists in the past, but there is no longer a reason for me to keep those. This book is the catch-all that will keep even the most hardcore thrill-seekers busy.

The *really* amazing thing? There are over 1000 great ideas here for any of us to grab that ever-so-necessary endorphin rush once in a while, yet the average person might only get to less than a handful of these in his or her entire lifetime. Personally, I was headed for that average route early on in life, and it only took one experience for me to realize that life held so much more than what is placed right in front of us on a daily basis. Taking that first step outside the box will open anybody's eyes to an incredible world of opportunities to test ourselves both physically and mentally, and in doing so, further us as human beings.

Many people think that these thrilling and non-traditional Things are a waste of time. Even more baffling are the people that think only fools partake in these adventures. Most often, it is fear speaking. This one emotion grips us in so many negative ways. Yet, you can use it to your advantage and begin to excel and go forward in life in a manner that cannot be described.

Ben has crafted a new version of the modern day self-help book. Although this is meant to be light reading, there really is a lot to be gained by knowing how these Things can affect a human being both physically and emotionally. Having this book in hand, there is no excuse for anybody not to try at least five of the thrills listed within one year. With the accurate difficulty-ranking system, you can start with the easy stuff—then gradually work your way up to a level that you consider *your* threshold for excitement.

We all have to take a leap of faith once in a while, and most of us certainly need to do it more often. If you are looking for the next adventure, whether it is training-intensive and pricey, or simply a quick, cheap thrill, it is definitely on this list. If for nothing else, *1001 Things to Do if You Dare* is a great read with some interesting knowledge being shared. I personally will be trying many of them, and although the author discourages it, I highly recommend others to do the same. I know deep down he does too, but like any smart American, doesn't want to get sued.

—Troy Hartman, winner of the 1997 X-Games,
host of MTV's *Senseless Acts of Video*,
and aerial stuntman

ACKNOWLEDGMENTS

Many awesome thanks to Paula Munier; first as my editor, then as my publisher, she assigned, suggested, or cajoled me into far too many Things in this book.

Praise for Shannon and Alex Grynkewich, especially Shannon, who's cooler, and gave me legal advice.

Congrats to my students Chris Stinson and Ashley Harper, who offered excellent suggestions, and to all my students at the Community College of Southern Nevada. Now go read something else, dammit.

A big shout-out to Matt and Dawn Lacy, who put things in perspective, and modeled certain craziness in this book.

While I could have written this without Wikipedia, it wouldn't have been nearly as easy.

My neighbors Sue and Bob Barr gave me plenty of input over cold beers on hot days.

Jane Francis seems as skeptical and cynical as me, which made for great entries to the list.

Andrew Harley, Wry, Travis Lippert, Walter Hollis, and the other yokels from *www.eDodo.org* gave me plenty of suggestions, a few of which were actually helpful.

And let's add Colonel David Hughes, USA (ret.), to that list of eDodo participants, but he also deserves his own special acknowledgment. Check out the true story of how he put Mount Everest on the World Wide Web by setting up the network at the Sherpa base camp himself—at the age of seventy-four (*www.linking*

everest.com). That's only one of the many astounding things Colonel Hughes has accomplished in his long life—I am in awe.

Doc, Joyce, and Phil Scheinman, who gave me far more advice than was strictly necessary.

Irving Ehrlich gave me the one about the dog's name, way back when.

Both Snopes.com and Cecil Adams with his "The Straight Dope" do far better for humanity than they will ever be paid for. I just wish more people would acknowledge them—or at least read them.

Scott Nishwitz told me about the practice of "mudding." That left me with mental images I've been forever unable to exorcise.

Steve Malisow and Craig Malisow got a bit whiny, but contributed nonetheless.

Jim Ebel took being my Hellmaster seriously, and that led to certain things that ended up in the book, one way or another.

Ryan and Kim Nankivel let me roll one of their ATVs—and then they got married afterward. Weird people. But great.

Sue Grant, for being a kickass writer, and for giving me advice on how to handle the financial end.

And Tim Lee, who rappelled off the dorm roof to clean his windows, "Because they were dirty." Dumbass.

INTRODUCTION

Many of the things in this book are dangerous. No, really—participating in some of these activities can lead to serious harm, permanent injury and disfigurement, or even death. Some of them are incredibly stupid, some are probably criminal in most locales, and some are just criminally stupid. The author has done some of these things; others he wouldn't do if you promised him cotton candy and sexual favors for a hundred years. The number of skulls ☠ following the activities listed in this book denotes the author's estimation of difficulty/insanity/stupidity of that particular item—1 for things that your grandmother could probably accomplish, 5 for things that are just ludicrously dangerous and inane.

The author, editors, publishers, and everyone affiliated with them do *not* recommend you try any of these, and, if you do, warn you that you do so at your own risk, and, furthermore, that we will have very little sympathy for you when you get hurt. We told you so.

There is something immensely satisfying, however, about participating in an activity that is inherently dangerous (and "dangerous" is used here not just to describe the possibility of physical harm, but psychological, emotional, and financial damage). There's the adrenaline rush, the view of one's own mortality, the welcome relief at the successful conclusion of the act. There is often a strange thrill of accomplishment, a self-congratulatory sensation, even when it's completely unwarranted (such as is earned by skydiving, which really isn't anything you, yourself, have done well, but is more a simple act of gravity and the expertise of the 'chute manufacturer).

We like to scare ourselves. We like to push our own boundaries. We like to take risks, sometimes even foolhardy ones.

Most people aren't aware that vertigo isn't really a fear of heights. Vertigo, instead, is a fear of edges. There is something tucked away at the base of our snake brain, some little sensor which has been honed over eons to protect the animal that carries it; this instinctual device screams at us when we're about to do something which is quite obviously a threat to life and limb. This alarm system lets you walk up to the edge. It will even let you peek over. But if you start to consider leaping, this ancient security protocol will scream at you, telling you that the action you're contemplating is quite ill-advised. It can fiddle with your psyche as well as your biology, causing a myriad of reactions, from uncontrollable panting to muscle spasms to realistic visions of tragic outcomes.

This thing is meant to protect you. You can have great fun by poking it a few times and telling it to get bent.

Pick an edge; an actual edge, like a cliff, or a waterfall, or pick a metaphorical edge, like the limits of your patience or bravery. Go up to that edge, peer out over. Let your safety mechanism tell you how silly you're acting. Then jump.

PART

1

public
things

Performing a daring Thing where someone can see you is perhaps more frightening than doing it somewhere free from view; there is the additional fear of embarrassment to hinder you.

Of course, depending on the audience, you may also get a group of people who egg you on.

SPEED, HEIGHT, DEPTH, AND MOTION THINGS

There's something almost universally thrilling about moving your body at high velocity . . . probably because it was never designed to do so.

☐ **1. Ride a roller coaster.**

☠

For an added thrill, do it without holding onto the restraints.

☐ **2. Drive a car.**

☠ ☠ ☠

Leading cause of death among American children. Think about that.

☐ **3. Drive the Autobahn.**

☠ ☠ ☠ ☠

A wide, well-maintained road with no speed limit? Mama, sign me up! The Autobahn winds through Switzerland, Austria, and Germany—and sure, in some places there are speed limits (and concessions made for conditions throughout), but it's mainly a megafreeway with no restrictions on your lead-foot instinct.

☐ 4. Bury the speedometer needle of a car.
☠ ☠ ☠ ☠

Take a vehicle somewhere desolate, where it would be impossible to harm another person (or somewhere it's allowed, like a racetrack). Rev it up, cut loose, and press the pedal all the way down. Keep it depressed until the speed indicator exceeds the highest number on the device. (As a challenge to the extra-stupid: Do this in a vehicle with a digital speedometer.)

☐ 5. Rev it all the way up and kick out the jams on a dry desert lakebed.
☠ ☠ ☠

The American Southwest has a big, beautiful desert, perfectly level, perfectly flat, perfect hardened by the sun and arid conditions. Make the most of it—it was created by years of natural development to be the optimum testing ground for your performance vehicle.

☐ 6. Drive a motor vehicle on a frozen lake.
☠ ☠ ☠ – ☠ ☠ ☠ ☠ ☠, depending on conditions

Lakes often freeze without uniformity—meaning some spots are usually softer/thinner/more brittle than others. Take a life vest.

❏ 7. Put a car up on two wheels.

☠ ☠ ☠ ☠ ☠

Okay, maybe you're so cool you can pull this off . . . but can you get it back down, on all four wheels?

❏ 8. Drive a truck.

☠ ☠ ☠

You've got a higher center of gravity, more gas in the tank, and a bigger engine. These can add up to trouble. Know what you're doing before you do it.

❏ 9. Drive a van.

☠ ☠ ☠

Forget the rearview mirror—it's useless. The only chance you have with peripherals and seeing anything behind you is constant use of the driver's-side mirror. It's a big, clunky, unwieldy vehicle, with low clearance and undersized wheels. More power to ya.

❏ 10. Drive a forklift.

☠ ☠ ☠

Those big prongs sticking out the front can really wallop someone or something, so be extra careful; even if you drive your car like an expert, it's tough to get a feel for where the front of the forklift actually is. Plus, if you're lucky, you get one of those forklifts equipped with rear wheels that turn, instead of the front set, making steering that much more tricky.

11. Drive a big honkin' piece of construction machinery.

☠ ☠ ☠ ☠

As children, many of us were fascinated with toy reproductions of giant earthmovers, bulldozers, cranes and such. That appreciation doesn't ever totally dwindle—we'd still get a massive kick out of sitting at the helm of one of those multistory monsters. Gimme.

12. Bungee jump.

☠ ☠ ☠

This was a practice originated by some South Pacific islanders, who were evidently incredibly bored with living in a glorious, unspoiled tropical paradise. Or they were under the influence of serious narcotics. My bet's on the latter. This is just plain stupid. I've had mixed results in my experiences with rubber bands . . . why would I trust one to withstand the weight of my body at terminal velocity?

13. BASE jump.

☠ ☠ ☠ ☠ ☠

Put on a parachute. Climb to the top of a Bridge, Antenna, Span, or mountain/hill/cliff (the E is "Earth"). Jump. Deploy parachute. Congratulations: You're officially nuts.

14. BASE jump from the "Tallest" something.

☠ ☠ ☠ ☠ ☠

The current World's Tallest Building. The Highest Bridge in America. The Most Steep Radio Tower in Lower East Missouri. Whatever. Make it count, so you can say you did it.

15. Skydive.
☠ ☠ ☠

Ahem. Humanity truly conquered the third dimension when the Wright brothers finally mastered the art of sustained, controlled, powered flight. Now, as a human being, you want to tempt nature by jumping out of that aircraft our species worked so hard to perfect? Are you out of your mind? I'm not.

16. Do a HALO jump.
☠ ☠ ☠ ☠

This is a High-Altitude, Low-Opening skydive. Go way, way, way up into the sky—say, 20,000 feet—jump out, freefall for a good, long while (and distance!), then pull the cord when you're way too close to the ground (usually under the 2,500-foot "floor" for normal parachuting). Be sure to bring oxygen, an altimeter, and some warm clothing.

17. Skydive out of a helicopter.
☠ ☠ ☠

It's got the capability to hover, which is kind of nifty, considering your purpose. Getting real altitude might be tricky, though.

18. Sky-surf.
☠ ☠ ☠

Skydiving—while standing on a board. I am not sure why there is so much focus on boards, when it comes to the various "extreme" sports. A latent construction fetish? The mind boggles.

❑ 19. Ride a motorcycle.

☠ ☠ ☠

Without a helmet. In traffic. In the rain. More than one rider will admit, sheepishly, after many drinks and some familiarity with the listener, that they've accomplished wondrous, crazy, awesome stunts on a bike, only to dump it while trying to park the damned thing.

❑ 20. Jump a motorcycle.

☠ ☠ ☠ ☠ ☠

For Fonzie Points, do it over a shark tank. To satisfy your historical/etymological jones, check out *www.jumptheshark.com.*

❑ 21. Pop a wheelie.

☠ – ☠ ☠ ☠ ☠ ☠, depending on vehicle

No, it doesn't have to be on a motorcycle; try a bicycle first, just to get the feel of the thing. Work up to other, bigger, more powerful rides.

❑ 22. Drive/ride/pilot an insanely high-powered vehicle for which you have no training whatsoever.

☠ ☠ ☠ ☠ ☠

Yeah, this was my buddy's Kawasaki Ninja 750, a massive sport bike that I had absolutely no business even sitting on, and outweighed me by a good 250 pounds. I had never been on a motorcycle before. I was proud that I navigated the suburban road at a wild 35 miles per hour, and returned to the driveway I'd started from. Then I dumped it trying to dismount.

23. Ride in a plane.

☠

If, in this century, you have not availed yourself of air travel, you are missing out on a full life.

24. Wingwalk.

☠ ☠ ☠ ☠ ☠

Some people used to do this on a regular basis, back in the early days of flying. They go up in a plane (almost always with an open cockpit/cabin), then get out and crawl/pull themselves along the outside surfaces of the aircraft, in a display of bravery and stupidity. I can't fathom the reasons why.

25. Fly a plane.

☠ ☠ ☠

Here's the dirty little secret pilots won't tell you: Flying a plane is easy. It's landing one that's damned hard. But taking up a plane, any kind of plane, for the first time, is righteously intense. Some have described it as "better than sex."

26. Try barnstorming.

☠ ☠ ☠ ☠ ☠

Not much call for this, nowadays, but it used to be all the rage. Take a small plane up into the air, and do insanely crazy "tricks" with it. This is currently somewhat akin to having the ability to wield a broadsword—it just doesn't come up that often.

27. Fly a plane across the Arctic, Australia, or the Antarctica.

☠ ☠ ☠ ☠ ☠

Commonly referred to as "bush flying." The word *bush*, in this context, means "place out in the middle of nowhere." There is no place safe to land, no services available, and you could, theoretically, wander indefinitely if forced to put down.

28. Fly a hang glider.

☠ ☠

See, most people would think this would be more dangerous than flying a plane, because there's no engine. Actually, that's what makes it safer: there's no high-tech moving parts to worry about, no fuel to burst into flame and incinerate the pilot, much fewer things to go wrong. Plus, it's a better ride: totally silent, except for the wind rushing past the canopy. Magic. Awesome.

29. Ride in a small jet with less than three seats.

☠ ☠ ☠

Pilots, especially jet pilots, especially Air Force jet pilots, are odd people, with a strange collective sense of humor. So they'll do things like tell you to look out the right side of the canopy, then yank the stick hard to snap your helmeted noggin into the other side of the canopy. They're weird creatures. Yes, they are.

30. Bail out of an aircraft with an ejection seat.

☠ ☠ ☠ ☠ ☠

Basically, you're sitting on a considerably high-powered explosive charge. When you fire that puppy, it's going to blast you into the air; if the aircraft is aloft, you're going to hit the airstream pretty much instantaneously, which is not like the mainly stationary air you feel around you most of the time. After all that, you've still got to hope the parachute opens, and that you land intact.

31. Ride in a helicopter.

☠ ☠ ☠

With the doors open. Over the hot New Mexico desert. In summer. After eating a full lunch, including chicken à la king. I'd never been airsick before, but that was too much for my stomach. Tried to hold it in the glove that came with my flight suit, too. I mean, you can't throw it out the window in a helicopter.

32. Go up in a hot air balloon.

☠

There are few dares more sedate at this altitude. The balloon's only going to go where the wind takes it, at the speed of the wind, so you're not really going to be cruising around all that much—especially if you're tethered, as many balloon rides are.

33. Go for a ride in a blimp.

☠

This is like a hot air balloon, only it has a propeller and control surfaces, so you can, like, steer it. Yee-haw.

1001 THINGS TO DO IF YOU DARE

❏ 34. Drive while exhausted.

☠ ☠ ☠ ☠ ☠ +

This is, diabolically, much more dangerous than driving inebriated. Especially at dusk, you may start to see the "wee beasties," phantoms of critters zooming onto the road from the distant shoulders, just on the edge of your peripheral vision. Spooky.

❏ 35. Crash a vehicle.

☠ ☠ ☠ ☠ ☠

Writers lie—time does not slow down when an accident is imminent; if it did, you'd be able to respond in time to avoid the collision. Instead, time kind of telescopes. . . .There's a brief jumble during the instant before the crash itself, then the crash, then there is a portion of time immediately subsequent in which the prior fifteen seconds or so are clearly delineated in your mind's eye, and you can zoom in and out on any given detail. It's weird. But if you walk away, what a rush!

❏ 36. Roll a car/truck.

☠ ☠ ☠ ☠ ☠

I've known only a couple people who have done this and survived. Most motor vehicles are not designed to go upside-down in any safe manner.

❏ 37. Drag race.

☠ ☠

There are racetracks that allow just anybody off the street to come in and try racing their own vehicles. Their insurance will probably cover anything that happens to them. Yours won't.

PART 1 PUBLIC THINGS

38. Drag race on a city street.

☠ ☠ ☠ ☠

Insanely dangerous stunt usually restricted to teenagers who have no sense of their own mortality.

39. Challenge a police interceptor to a drag race.

☠ ☠ ☠ ☠ ☠

Hey, cops are people, too. Some of them joined the force for the express purpose of driving in a crazy fashion. You never know just which ones might want to indulge your deranged ambitions. Remember—their car is much better than yours.

40. Conduct a point-to-point race with automobiles.

☠ ☠ ☠

Much more fun—and, realistically, more challenging—than a quarter-mile drag. The route is the thing, so knowledge of the terrain is key. One of the few times where age and wisdom will triumph over youth and excellent motor skills.

41. Cross the street without looking.

☠ ☠ ☠ ☠

You know how everyone told you not to do this when you were growing up? There's good reason for that.

42. Cross a New York City street in front of a bus.

☠ ☠ ☠ ☠ ☠

Pure and unadulterated suicide.

☐ 43. Cross a Las Vegas street outside of a crosswalk.

☠ ☠ ☠ ☠

One of the few places on the planet where you will be cited, posthumously, for jaywalking, if a vehicle does indeed strike you dead. Sure, pedestrians still have the right of way, no matter what, no matter where, but law enforcement in this rather libertarian town frowns on those who cross against the light (or anywhere other than in prescribed locations). As long as the driver doesn't flee the scene, they're likely to get off with a stern warning and a slap on the wrist—while you, the pedestrian, are likely to be sundered.

☐ 44. Learn to drive a vehicle with a manual transmission.

☠

Driving stick is cool. It just is. You have control over the vehicle, you can change gears in a more efficient, faster manner, blah-blah-blah. It's just cool. That's all there is to it.

☐ 45. Drive in a foreign country.

☠ ☠

The rules are pretty much the same on roads everywhere in the world. It's not the rules you have to worry about—it's the accepted practices. There are nuances to driving, things all drivers in a certain place just happen to know, but aren't posted on any sign or in any rulebook. Don't look for help at the rental car desk, either. Try not to kill anyone. Or be killed, of course.

❏ 46. Drive a vehicle with a manual transmission in a foreign country.

☠ ☠

Suddenly, all those reflexes you've honed over the years, all the capability you so ably demonstrate back at home, flees from your body. I don't know why this is. I think maybe it's something that they do to you when they stamp your passport. The locals will certainly not be forgiving of your lapses.

❏ 47. Drive on the wrong side of the road.

☠ ☠ ☠

The place where you grew up will dictate which side of the road is comfortable for you. Foreign countries sometimes mess with that instinct, purposefully, to confuse tourists. Okay—maybe it's not intentional. But it may as well be.

❏ 48. Drive a vehicle with a manual transmission in a foreign country on the wrong side of the road.

☠ ☠ ☠

Wait—who's got the right of way? Can I make a left on red? What the—what the f--k was that? Who's honking? Got—to—shift—with my subordinate hand. Oh—wait—signal—s--t! That's the windshield wipers!

❏ 49. Drive the wrong way down a one-way street.

☠ ☠ ☠

1001 THINGS TO DO IF YOU DARE

Sometimes—just sometimes, mind you—there are places you have to be, in cities expressly designed to keep you from getting to them. Sometimes circumstances conspire to make your destination unreachable. Sometimes you just have to decide to dismiss convention and legality, and just get to where you're going by going the wrong way. Oddly, many of the opposing drivers are very forgiving. Don't let this give you false security; remain wary until you actually get where you're going.

❏ 50. Enter a highway via the off-ramp (or exit via the on-ramp).

☠ ☠ ☠

There was an accident. Or a large event that is about to begin or has just ended. The roads pointed in a certain direction are jammed beyond capacity. You must get on (or off) the highway—it is essential. The only possible route is prohibited by law and common sense. Go slow, but get it done and get out of there.

❏ 51. Learn to drive a tractor-trailer rig.

☠ ☠ ☠

There's something about double-clutching involved, I think. That's the practice of using an unsynchronized manual transmission. There's also the necessity of an engine brake (called a "Jake brake") and/or air brakes, as truck braking systems don't use hydraulics. I know it's not just the same as driving a regular car. At least, I don't think so. Anyway, it seems pretty tricky. There are special schools for it and everything.

❏ 52. Pilot a seated personal watercraft.

☠

This looks a lot tougher than it actually is. Fortunately, it is just about as much fun as it looks, too. What could be simpler? Sit down, hit the gas, and fly across the water. Even if you wipe out, you're only going to hit the water, and you're not really going fast enough for it to hurt. Well, most of the time.

❏ 53. Pilot an upright personal watercraft.

☠ ☠

A little tougher than a wet bike; with a standup model, you've got to actually exert some effort. You're also a lot more apt to guzzle an annoying volume of water.

❏ 54. Go sailing.

☠ ☠

Yep—plop yourself into a transportation vehicle that utilizes an accelerant that has been used by our species for thousands of years. It has been used more or less successfully and safely. It's actually kind of fun—until you have to paddle or drag it in when the wind dies.

❏ 55. Sail a homemade watercraft, built strictly from naturally occurring materials, from one side of the ocean to the other.

☠ ☠ ☠ ☠ ☠

That Thor Heyerdahl guy did it. Doesn't mean you can. Thor was a tough, smart Scandinavian, with a background in marine biology and anthropology. Odds are, you aren't.

Jump from a moving . . .

❑ 56. . . . bicycle.

☠

Something kids do, because, well, they're kids. Most often, the bike keeps going and you don't. Tuck and roll.

❑ 57. . . . car.

☠ ☠ ☠

Usually, this is on pavement, so you're quite apt to shatter some portion of your skeletal structure by cracking it hard against the street. Not for the faint of heart.

❑ 58. . . . train.

☠ ☠ ☠ ☠ ☠

A lot more lethal than depicted in popular media. An almost sure-fire way of taking care of any problems associated with that pastime known as "living."

❑ 59. . . . watercraft.

☠ ☠ ☠ ☠ ☠

We like to think that water is a nice shock absorber, that it's in some ways soft and gentle. Okay, maybe it's softer than concrete— but that doesn't make it actually soft, especially when you hit it with any considerable speed. Plus, if the concussion of the impact stuns, immobilizes, or knocks you unconscious, you drown.

❑ 60. Ride a riptide.

☠ ☠ ☠

Large bodies of water do funny things. For instance, they sometimes create riptides, strong currents of water capable of dragging something fairly large and semibuoyant (you) from near the shore out to deeper waters. You can try to fight and probably drown, or you can go with it and enjoy the trip, then swim carefully, parallel to the shore, back to the beach. Your choice.

61. Race a go-cart.

Quite possibly the stupidest activity one could ever opt to try. It's a miniature car that goes slower than a real car, in a more stable fashion. What the hell kind of dare is that? Dumb, dumb, dumb. I guess it'd be fun for kids.

62. Go over a waterfall.

depending on conditions

The Thing of mythic proportions is the ride over Niagara Falls in a barrel. It is also a pretty sure-fire way to off yourself. So, unless you're looking for a flamboyant means of self-euthanizing, you might want to start with a tiny little waterfall of six feet or so, in a boat, while wearing a life jacket. You can work up to the life-threatening ones; they'll still be there when you're ready to die.

63. Go over Niagara.

Plain dumb. Nobody ever survived a plunge over American Falls, but a few have made it down Horseshoe Falls.

☐ 64. Drive through a blowout; pull over safely.
☠ ☠

You might not even hear the bang; if you do, it might just sound like you ran over a rock, or some debris was kicked up into the wheel well. The blowout itself might not be apparent until you start losing control of the vehicle, or you smell the rubber burning. The steering becomes mushy and unresponsive and the vehicle strays. This is not pleasant in traffic and/or when traveling at a high rate of speed.

☐ 65. Change a tire.
☠

You may find yourself enjoying a strangely disproportionate amount of satisfaction, as if you'd accomplished the modern equivalent of fording a river in an ox-drawn cart. Get over yourself.

☐ 66. Change a tire on the side of the freeway.
☠ ☠

Make damned sure you've got the jack positioned properly. The slipstream of large vehicles, moving quickly, are definitely going to rock your wounded transport as it looms over you. Semis are the worst; you'll swear that you're about to be sucked right into traffic. Cough through the exhaust and do what you gotta.

☐ 67. Change a tire on the side of the freeway in a foreign country.
☠ ☠ ☠

All of the regular fun associated with this activity, with the added pleasure of knowing that you now have a giant target painted on your ass, along with the words "Stupid Tourist in Peril." Might as well just be transmogrified into a bird with a broken wing shuffling outside a snake's den.

☐ 68. Ride a cigarette boat.
☠ ☠ ☠

You know these things: the type of watercraft that drug smugglers like to use. You're not so much riding across the waves as skipping across them, like a stone flung sideways. And, like that stone, you can tip sideways and flip repeatedly.

☐ 69. Go down into a defunct mine.
☠ ☠ ☠

It's dirty, dusty, dank, and dark. And damned dangerous. The ceiling could fall in at any time, and then your goose is truly cooked.

☐ 70. Go down into an active mine.
☠ ☠ ☠ ☠

There's a reason why this is no longer the job of choice for migrant workers. But, hey, if your professional skills amount to digging, then this is probably your best bet.

☐ 71. Go underwater in a submarine.
☠ ☠ – ☠ ☠ ☠ ☠, depending on circumstances
Sure, when you're diving, there's just as much chance something could go wrong . . . but you're probably deeper in the submarine.

And you're trapped inside. There are just a few places where a tourist can find a submarine to ride: There's a provider called Atlantis Adventures (which spooks me, 'cause I remember where the term *Atlantis* comes from), Disneyland, and—formerly—the Edmonton Mall. Edmonton yanked theirs in 1998, so hurry and get to one of the others, before they decide to cancel the offer, too.

❑ 72. Go down into the ocean in a nuclear submarine.

☠ ☠ ☠ ☠

A bit more dramatic than your basic aqua-park minisub ride. Of course, the only way to accomplish this, really, is to join either the Russian or American Navy, neither of which may appeal to you.

❑ 73. Go investigate the Marianas Trench in some sort of submersible vehicle.

☠ ☠ ☠ ☠ ☠

Supposedly the "deepest" place in the ocean—and, therefore, the lowest point on the planet, short of piercing Earth's crust. When looking for Daring Things, activities that end in *est* are always good choices. The bottom of the trench, known as the Challenger Deep, is supposedly as far below sea level as Mount Everest is above it. This one, of course, comes with a very definite possibility of being crushed by the massive pressure water exerts at great depths.

74. Go off-roading.

☠ ☠

There's a reason we have roads. Roads are good: They are, for the most part, level, flat, and smooth, and engineered to support the weight of automobiles. Once you go off-roading, well, you're going off the road. In a vehicle. Which really isn't the purpose of the vehicle, nor the nonroad part of the planet. Hopefully, you've got roll bars. And plenty of drinking water.

75. Go off-roading through the desert.

☠ ☠ ☠

Lots of sand; big, well-treaded tires and a high-clearance chassis will help. So will a winch, for when you get stuck. Because you will get stuck. Bring more water than usual.

76. Go off-roading in the mud.

☠ ☠ ☠

There are people for whom this is fun on a regular basis. They even have a name for the practice: "mudding." Okay, so maybe they're not all that creative, but they seem to find amusement easily. The concept of mudding seems to be this: take a huge, overpowered truck out to a muddy area, and try as hard as possible to get it stuck. There you go. Mudding. Yep.

77. Ride a snowmobile.

☠ ☠ – ☠ ☠ ☠ ☠ ☠,

depending on circumstances

Only Americans would come up with the idea of plunking the

internal combustion engine into a tracked vehicle to scoot across the snow. It was a Wisconsinite who came up with this notion (and the very best people, as we all know, come from Wisconsin). Carl Eliason got the first patent for his converted Model T Ford in 1927. The most powerful snowmobiles can now also skim across the water if the speed is high enough, but even this book doesn't recommend something as insane as that.

78. Drive an all-terrain vehicle (ATV).

☠ ☠ – ☠ ☠ ☠ ☠ ☠,
depending on circumstances

The scourge of parents and environmentalists. A small, highly maneuverable, fast machine, designed to conquer any form of land, in all seasons (hence the name).

79. Roll an ATV.

☠ ☠ ☠ ☠ – ☠ ☠ ☠ ☠ ☠

Even though they are squat vehicles, with a low center of gravity, and some have four wheels in a rectangular configuration, these are still not the most stable of platforms. You can flip one, sure as s--t; often, without trying. Depending on the size of the thing, getting it upright again can be tricky. . . . Before attempting, make sure it's on a flat piece of terrain; this is not always easy, because it's quite likely that the reason you flipped was that you weren't on flat terrain. Stand off to the side—don't straddle it like a fallen motorcycle. Grab somewhere solid, and rock that sucker back up. Don't pull too hard, or you'll end up underneath it as it rolls all the way over.

80. Go on a ride at a traveling carnival.

☠☠☠ – ☠☠☠☠☠,

depending on circumstances

I can't understand why it is that recreational amputation is illegal, while this activity is still allowed. Look at these devices: Is it even possible that they're all sufficiently maintained and insured? Look at the people responsible for operating them. Would you allow them to even park your car? This is ludicrous.

81. Walk a tightrope.

☠☠☠

Let's look at this with a perfectly objective eye: It's a string, tied between two points suspended above the ground. A person is going to walk across it. Now walking, if you ask any biologist, is not a real means of locomotion; walking is instead considered repetitive, controlled falling. Get that? Falling. You're going to fall across a string, some distance above the ground? Sure, you can take lessons, if you want. Try Flying Trapeze Chicago; you can reach them via their Web site, *www.flyingtrapezechicago.com.*

82. Walk on a ledge between two buildings, or two rooms of a building.

☠☠☠☠

Extremely similar to the foolishness of a tightrope, but here you have the added benefits of a structure wholly inappropriate for the purpose. For extra insanity, try it in the rain or wind or snow. I had a college roommate who rappelled off the top of the dorm building to wash the outside windows of his fourth-floor dorm room. Why? "Because they were dirty," he explained. Of course.

83. Pilot an ultralight.

☠ ☠ ☠ ☠

Remember what I said about hang gliders? Well, this is a hang glider with a lawnmower engine strapped to a basket hanging underneath it; you're supposed to sit in the basket and zoom along with the lawnmower engine pushing you. Through the air. Currently, the Federal Aviation Administration regulates the operation of these vehicles (under Title 14, Part 103). You have been warned.

84. Windsail an iceboat across a frozen body of water.

☠ ☠ ☠

Yeah, it's sort of like a sled, and sort of like a sailboat. You sit on it, let the sail grab the wind, and go skidding across the ice. Where might they want to do it? The answers, as is so often the case, are "Wisconsinites" and "Wisconsin," of course! Places like Mendota, and Waubesa, and Monona. Which are not punch lines—they are cities. Or lakes. Or something.

85. Pilot an airboat.

☠ ☠ ☠

This is popular down in Cajun country, that part of the South where swamps and muck and mosquitoes are the mainstay. By slapping a giant fan onto the back of a raft, you are able to pilot across the surface of marshlands, so that you can get to . . . whatever it is you do in the swamps. Quickly.

PART 1 PUBLIC THINGS

86. Get shot out of a cannon.

☠ ☠ ☠ ☠ ☠

Explosives aren't really featured in this activity, but they might as well be. Riding a shove from compressed air or an elastic slingshot, the human cannonball flies through the air to—hopefully—land in a net. There are easier ways to kill yourself.

87. Walk the high iron.

☠ ☠ ☠

There's some construction going on; someone's putting up a tall building, which rises several hundred feet above the ground. The dudes up at the top of it, the ones who actually shape the skeleton that the rest of the facility will take for support, those are the ironworkers. They are the ninjas of the construction trade. If you're very nice to them, they may let you go up and walk around up there.

88. Climb a tree.

☠ – ☠ ☠ ☠ ☠ ☠,

depending on species and conditions

Yes, it may be a bit childish. (Have you been reading this f--king list? Almost everything in here requires a degree of immaturity unknown among even a tribe of howler monkeys.) Anyway, climbing a tree is a lot of fun. I recommend avoiding the coniferous varieties, as the resin and nettles take a lot of the enjoyment out of the experience. The higher you can go in one of these mothers, the better. For extra thrills, try a redwood or sequoia.

❐ 89. Build a tree house.

☠ ☠ ☠

This is the traditional means to "get away from it all." And with good reason: up in a tree, you can feel very isolated and distinct from other members of the species (humans don't often occupy treetops). It's a tough logistical challenge, as all trees are different, so there are no standardized blueprints for tree houses, but it's well worth it.

❐ 90. Sleep overnight in a tree house.

☠ ☠ ☠ ☠

Tricky. Sure, it's fairly quiet and peaceful, what with the winds in the leaves and whatnot, but you sure don't want to wake up on the wrong side of the bed. . . .

❐ 91. Live in a tree house.

☠ ☠ ☠ ☠ ☠

There are, in fact, people who do this. Try not to think about their plumbing arrangements.

❐ 92. Live in a tree house as a protest.

☠ ☠ ☠ ☠ ☠

Anger lumberjacks, law enforcement officials, and those who care about you. Or the people you'd want mad at you. . . .

❐ 93. Jump out a window.

☠ – ☠ ☠ ☠ ☠ ☠, depending on height

Notice I didn't say "jump through a window," because that's just suicidal, no matter how it's presented in the popular media.

❏ 94. Jump through a window.

☠ ☠ ☠ ☠ ☠ +

Did you not understand the word suicidal?

ATHLETIC THINGS

The human body is an amazing tool. On the one hand, it's an incredibly durable, time-tested vehicle for survival, capable of withstanding ridiculous amounts of punishment and privation. On the other hand, it's very delicate, and can be rendered inoperable through any number of relatively innocuous means.

We like to explore the limits of the body's capacity for pain, exertion, and stress; we call this "athleticism." Push your own body through a series of activities that force it to the extreme parameters of endurance, neglect, and determination.

INDIVIDUAL THINGS

There is something liberating about doing something challenging without a lot of other people standing around, waiting for you to screw up. There's less pressure. Of course, the flip side is that there is also nobody rooting for you, and encouragement can also give you that extra edge to accomplish something.

❏ 95. Downhill (Alpine) skiing.

☠ – ☠ ☠ ☠ ☠ ☠, depending on conditions

The cold wind abrading your cheekbones. The crunch and slice of the underside of your skis as they cleave your path down the run. The muffled thud and twirl and tumble as you fall on your

ass. Still one of the most enjoyable things to do, if you can find any talent for it.

❏ 96. Ski down a double black diamond run in the Rocky Mountains.

☠ ☠ ☠ ☠

These ain't your dinky Appalachian Smokys. Not some floofy European Alps. These are the no-kidding, gonna-kill-ya, 17,000-foot dagger-toothed monsters. They mean business. But with the altitude and the Colorado sun, you might be able to do it comfortably in jeans and a windbreaker. Cool.

❏ 97. Snowboarding.

☠ ☠

This pastime was devised specifically to make anyone over the age of seventeen look like an idiot, and fall on their ass the entire day. It works. It's just silly, but the kids seem to like it; snowboarding is growing in popularity, adding annoying teens to lift lines the world over.

❏ 98. Wakeboarding.

☠ ☠ ☠

An abomination—the deranged hybrid of skateboarding, water-skiing, surfing, and snowboarding. You've got a board—your feet are strapped to it. You grab a rope attached to a motorboat. The boat takes off. Theoretically, you go zipping along behind. More likely, you're left floundering in the water, a good ways behind the boat.

❏ 99. Mountain-boarding.

☠ ☠

Yep. Mountain-boarding. For when there's no snow, of course. Addicts needed a way to fulfill their boarding jones even in July, so some clever person stuck a few wheels on a giant skateboard, and now participants can scoot down a mountain of dirt, sans snow.

❏ 100. Dive off a thirty-foot cliff into a freshwater lake.

☠

Two things make Canada tolerable, now that *Kids in the Hall* is off the air: Bob the Angry Flower (*www.angryflower.com*), and cliff-diving into a cool wilderness lake. And I've heard Bob is moving to the States.

❏ 101. Participate in a Competitive Apnea event.

☠ ☠

No, it's not about sleep apnea, which is something completely different (both terms come from a Greek word meaning "to breathe"; sleep apnea is when you have trouble breathing at night). But it does sound like a brain disease, doesn't it? And maybe it should be classified as such: Apnea covers a spectrum of competitions based around the practice of holding your breath underwater. I think they do it underwater so you can't cheat.

❏ 102. Try Static Apnea.

☠

Get this: a bunch of people get into a swimming pool, go underwater, and see how long they can hold their breath. Last one to surface wins. I think I played this when I was eight or nine, but nobody referred to it as a sporting event.

❏ 103. Try Dynamic Apnea.
☠ ☠

See how far you can swim underwater, using only one breath—the one who travels the most distance, wins.

❏ 104. Try Constant-Weight Apnea.
☠ ☠ ☠

See how deep you can swim without external equipment to help you sink. The person who goes deepest, wins.

❏ 105. Try Free-Immersion Apnea.
☠ ☠ ☠ ☠

A line is sunk into a body of water, way, way down. You try to go as deep as you can using the line, and then come back up.

❏ 106. Try Variable Weight Apnea.
☠ ☠ ☠ ☠

A weight apparatus drags you down as far as you want to go—then you come up using a line.

❏ 107. Try No-Limits Apnea.
☠ ☠ ☠ ☠ ☠

You use the weight thingy to go down as far as you want, then come back up with a personal floatation device. Crazy.

❏ 108. Go bodysurfing in the ocean.

☠

The ocean doesn't play around. It's not your friend—it doesn't care about you. Your ancestors left it about 400 million years ago, and it's never forgotten that slight. Why should it? Did you ever write? Or call? No, you thankless chump. So the ocean ain't gonna be nice to you, either. You quickly become aware of that fact when it grabs you, drags you under, churns you up a bit, and spits you out onto shore. But man, is that fun! An inexpensive entertainment, as long as you live near an ocean.

❏ 109. Ride a surfboard.

☠ – ☠ ☠ ☠ ☠ ☠, depending on conditions
Knees, balance, and a digestive tract resistant to constant forceful ingestion of seawater. Remember, to a shark, the bottom of the board will always look like a tasty seal.

❏ 110. Try kite-surfing.

☠ ☠ ☠

Like demented followers of a Ben Franklin cult, these people fly a kite while surfing. The kite drags them across the water and high up into the air, allowing them to do crazier things than if they were just surfing. Where's lightning when you need it?

❏ 111. Try sailboarding.

☠ ☠

A surfboard with a sail attached. Because, y'know, you might want to surf from Here to There.

❏ 112. Swim against the current of a river.
☠ ☠

The river moves; that's what rivers do. They move. They, themselves, move, and they move stuff, too. They move a whole bunch of stuff. Rocks, dirt, mountains. See that Grand Canyon thingy? That was the work of a river. You think the river's going to have much problem moving you? What do you think you are? A salmon? You're not a salmon.

❏ 113. Swim the Mighty Mississip'.
☠ ☠ ☠

Any time you see the word *river* associated with any of the Things in this book, you can give yourself the extra added challenge of performing that act in, under, through, or over the Mississippi. The Big Muddy is the baddest piece of motile water in North America, and it is more than ready for your feeble efforts to best it.

❏ 114. Swim the Amazon.
☠ ☠ ☠ ☠

The Mississippi with piranhas and anacondas. Yes, piranhas. Which, supposedly, don't often attack people. But why take the chance? The Amazon carries more water, per year, than the Mississippi, Nile, and Yangtze put together. Yowza.

❏ 115. Swim the Nile.
☠ ☠ ☠ ☠ ☠

Arguably longer than the Amazon, with crocodiles and hippos.

116. Swim the English Channel.

☠ ☠ ☠ ☠ ☠

This is a devastating, harsher-than-death ordeal, chock-full of possible ways to destroy your body and mind. And it's really cold.

117. Swim beneath an underwater obstacle of indeterminate length.

☠ ☠ ☠ – ☠ ☠ ☠ ☠ ☠,

depending on distance and circumstances

Find out just how long you can hold your breath. Feel your lungs rebel against the tyranny of your idiocy. Let your sinuses attack your skull in various ways. Make sure you get to the other side of whatever it is you're swimming under.

118. Swim through the subterranean cavern at the Toilet Bowl in Hanauma Bay.

☠ ☠ ☠

On the island of Oahu, at a place called Hanauma Bay, a fluke of tidal erosion created a small basin that fills and empties according to some pattern of the waves. You can jump in while it's empty, then let the force of the incoming water eject you back onto the rock shelf surrounding the pool. A short distance away from the "bowl" itself, there's a fissure in the rocks, which leads to a small grotto, and a cavern that leads into the pool, underground and underwater. If you time it wrong, the wave action can thump you around within the narrow, submerged causeway pretty violently.

119. Do a "polar bear" swim.

☠

Pick a really cold place, during the cold season. Get up early in the morning, and go out to a body of water large enough to immerse yourself. Take off your clothes (leave your shoes on, or your feet will stick to the rocks on the way out). Jump in. Get out, dry off, and go home.

120. Swim in Lake Tahoe.

☠ ☠

Other, better writers than I have lauded the merits of Tahoe. They're all correct. Try to stay on the Nevada side. California sucks.

121. Go snorkeling.

☠ – ☠ ☠ ☠, depending on conditions

The snorkel is an awesome invention, allowing a swimmer/diver to look down into the water and still breathe. It can also funnel saltwater directly into your throat and lungs. Know what you're doing.

122. Climb a mountain.

☠

"Because it's there," ranks up there with the World's Stupidest Reasons, along with "Because I said so," and "It's the right thing to do." But some of us still get berated into doing things like this (and this thing, in particular), even knowing how inane it is.

123. Climb Everest.

☠ ☠ ☠ ☠ ☠

That's the Big Boy on the block. The topper. The boss. After that, what're you gonna do?

124. Run down the mountain afterward, as fast as possible.

☠ ☠

Boy, that mountain was high, wasn't it? Sure was. And it took us longer to get up it than we thought it would. Hey, check it out: It's getting cold. And dark. And I'm hungry. Y'know . . . it's going to be awfully tough to climb down this thing in the dark. . . .

125. Alternatively, rappel off the mountain.

☠ ☠ ☠

Go back and read the introduction to this book. See the part about walking up to the edge of the cliff? The part about your mind telling your body that this is a really, really bad idea? Okay. So you know already. So why are you doing this? If you're going to do it, no matter what, try to ensure that your "Swiss Seat" (the knotted-rope sling you use to support yourself on the descent) doesn't carve up your genitalia.

126. Better still, rappel off the mountain, Aussie-style (facing the ground).

☠ ☠ ☠

Here's where your belay team, those folks on the ground holding the tether-end of your rappel rope, really show their true character. When you're going backwards, you can't see them, so you don't know if they're just pretending to watch out for your safety, or cracking jokes and not paying any attention at all. Well, with this technique you get to actually see if they care about you or not. That's a dubious merit.

☐ 127. Rappel out of a helicopter.
☠ ☠

Surprisingly, this is a lot easier than the rappelling involving a mountain. There's no edge, especially if you start the activity by sitting in the open doorway of the chopper, your legs dangling out into space. You're looking down at the ground where you started (before the helicopter lifted off), but, after a hundred feet or so, you don't really have any concept of height—your depth perception doesn't work like that. So jumping is easy. Make sure to bark the "Hut-hut-hut" sounds from *The Blues Brothers* as you do it. Just check to see that the rope reaches the ground before you leap; if it does, landing is easy.

☐ 128. Climb a rock.
☠ ☠

"Rock climbing" generally means climbing an area of near-vertical, rocky elevation. It can be a part of mountain climbing, but some folks just look at a rock wall and think, "Hey, wouldn't it be cool to climb up that." I am not sure why.

☐ 129. Climb a boulder ("bouldering").
☠ ☠

Yeah. A boulder is a giant rock (bigger than you, anyway), standing all alone by itself. For some people, this means that it is just begging to be climbed.

130. Climb a building ("buildering").

☠ – ☠ ☠ ☠ ☠, depending on conditions

Every now and then, some a--hole in a crazy costume (often comic book hero Spiderman) tries to climb one of the world's tallest buildings. You, too, can be an a--hole. Just pick a building and start climbing. Buildings that have been climbed by various a--holes: the Sears Tower, the Sydney Opera House, the Eiffel Tower, the Empire State Building, and the National Bank of Abu Dhabi. This is usually illegal, and will result in your arrest. If you survive.

131. Climb a glacier ("ice climbing").

☠ ☠ ☠ ☠

This is a lot like rock climbing or mountain climbing, but with the added thrill of the possibilities of hidden fissures, instant fractures, ice avalanches, freezing to death, and lots and lots of snow. Superfun.

132. Climb a sea stack ("stack climbing").

☠ ☠ ☠

Sometimes, the vagaries of geology work out such that a strip of coastline is left hanging out into the water, like a mini-peninsula. Then, sometimes, the forces of erosion cut it up even more, and leave only a large column of rock and dirt sticking up out of the water. This is called a sea stack, and some people think climbing them is fun. I'm not one of them.

☐ 133. Try elevator surfing.
☠ ☠ ☠ ☠ ☠

Get inside an elevator shaft, and scramble on top of an elevator car. Ride around like that. As far as I can tell, that is pretty much the extent of elevator surfing.

☐ 134. Learn to juggle.
☠

This requires a lot of hand-eye coordination. And a lot of patience. A lot more than I have. And I don't really think it impresses potential sexual partners, so I don't really know what good it is. Interesting note, though: The most common form is "toss juggling," wherein objects are thrown into the air, and caught. Yes, there are different kinds of juggling. But they all involve jugglers.

☐ 135. Juggle sharp objects.
☠ ☠ ☠ ☠

Because nothing is nearly as impressive as slicing open your flesh in front of strangers.

☐ 136. Run a footrace.
☠ ☠

Who's the fastest human being present? Whoever runs fastest, of course. I, personally, run fastest when being chased, so the footrace thing hasn't really worked for me in the past.

❏ 137. Run competitive cross-country.
☠ ☠ ☠

Instead of a road or a track, participants must run over natural obstacles and terrain; this can get messy and awkward.

❏ 138. Run until you hit your absolute point of exhaustion.
☠ ☠ ☠

Keep running. Run until you vomit. Keep running. Then stop. Okay, this sounds really stupid. And, on the face of it, it is. But there's real value to this activity. Knowing your limit is intrinsically valuable. Knowing you can exceed it—and survive—is eminently more valuable.

❏ 139. Run a marathon.
☠ ☠ ☠ ☠

Somebody, hundreds of years ago, picked an arbitrary distance, a distance which the human body was not designed to travel quickly or comfortably, and made it a fad.

❏ 140. Go barefoot.
☠ – ☠ ☠ ☠ ☠, depending on conditions

Our feet aren't really equipped to be without some kind of protective covering for any length of time—hell, we aren't even really designed to walk upright continually, but that's another problem altogether. Anyway, our feet are delicate and sensitive, chock-full of bones, but with only a thin strip of skin and flesh securing them. The pads of our feet are not like that of other animals, with tough, fibrous material, able to withstand punishment—we are prone to becoming hobbled from slight injury. But if you get the chance to wander around without anything on your tootsies, you might find it amusing to feel the ground, and all its benefits and foibles, without something separating you from it. This is best over a nice, lush, dense grass, where the worst effect will be some severe tickling.

☐ 141. Go barefoot in an urban setting.
☠ ☠

Pavement is not that easy on feet (or knees, or ankles, or . . .). Add in the thrilling possibilities of broken glass, scrap metal, and abandoned chewing gum (among other sundry painful and disgusting obstacles), and you have quite the worthy Thing. Remember Bruce Willis in *Die Hard*? Like that.

☐ 142. Go barefoot in a wintry setting.
☠ ☠ ☠ ☠

Ice and snow don't complement human flesh. In addition to the threats of frostbite and abrasion, your extremities (in which your feet are included) radiate a great deal of body heat, and you can easily end up with a good case of hypothermia, which is a pretty straightforward way to die.

☐ 143. Ride a horse. For more fun, ride it at a gallop.
☠ ☠

This is a large animal, moving quickly. A very large animal. A very large, stupid animal. Hell, most dogs would consider a horse plain dumb. But remember—we measure machines in terms of horsepower. There's a reason for that.

❑ 144. Jump a horse.

☠☠ – ☠☠ ☠☠ ☠☠, depending on conditions

No—there's no way you can jump over a horse. I mean you should ride the horse over a jump, of course. People have been doing this for a long time—and horses have been doing it even longer. So it's nothing new. But if it's new for you, it's pretty wild.

❑ 145. Try the steeplechase.

☠☠ ☠☠ ☠☠

Here, you get to combine the most difficult aspects of riding a horse and jumping a horse. No kidding, this is really dangerous. And I'm not even sure the horses like it all that much. It's a horserace that involves all sorts of dangerous obstacles, including jumps and water pits. You might want to skip breakfast.

❑ 146. Play pato.

☠☠ ☠☠ ☠☠ ☠☠

How do I explain? . . . Okay. This is a combination of basketball and polo. Two teams of horseback riders try to grab a ball that has handles on it, carry it over to an elevated basket, and throw it through. All while staying on the horse. Really. Go to Argentina if you don't believe me—it's their national sport. Here's the best part: Originally, the game was not played with a ball, but with a duck in a basket. A duck! In a basket!

❏ 147. Play buzkashi.

☠ ☠ ☠ ☠

Very, very similar to pato, but played with the carcass of a goat instead of a ball, and violence is a crucial ingredient in the gameplay. The national sport of Afghanistan. Surprise.

❏ 148. Joust.

☠ ☠ ☠ ☠

You ride a horse carrying a lance (read: a large spear), and gallop full-tilt in one direction. Someone else on a horse, who also has a spear, gallops at you. You try to knock the other person off his or her horse, while the other rider tries to do the same to you. If you do this, you deserve whatever happens to you. You'll probably have to join a Renaissance Fair or the Society for Creative Anachronism to participate.

❏ 149. Ride a camel.

☠

You know what they say about camels, how they're smelly, obnoxious, annoying, irritable, contentious, stubborn, ugly beasts? That's all true. Have fun!

❏ 150. Ride a llama. Or alpaca.

☠

These things are all fluffy and soft and stuff. Really mild mannered and docile. Sweet creatures, really. The Middle East should band together to import an entire breeding stock of these, and get to work letting them evolve into a species that

PART 1 PUBLIC THINGS

can survive long periods of time without water. Of course, they'd probably turn into camels.

151. Ride an ostrich.

I don't know why anyone would want to do this. I mean, it's a bird. Why would you want to ride a bird? That's silly. And the ostrich knows it's silly. The ostrich will be glad to let you know how silly it is. According to North Dakota State University, an adult ostrich can kick with 500 pounds of pressure per square inch. Several sources suggest that one person per year, from 1997 to 2000, was killed by ostriches. And how silly would you feel if you were killed by an ostrich?

152. Ride a wild burro.

See "Ride a camel." Wild burros are even more dangerous. You can find them plentifully scattered across the American Southwest.

153. Ride an elephant.

The elephant is the largest land animal on Earth. You don't even come close. Keep that in mind. Many jurisdictions across the country are banning elephant rides at parks, zoos, and circuses to prevent injuries and/or deaths caused by rampaging elephants. They might be on to something.

❏ 154. Use an elephant to herd rhinos.
☠ ☠ ☠ ☠ ☠

I saw a film of this actually happening. Nepalese National Park service rangers got up on elephants and used them to herd a rhino into the open, where it could be shot with a tranquilizer gun. Hysterical . . . except, probably, for the rhino. You can contact the BBC if you want to try to get a copy of the film.

❏ 155. Ride a yak.
☠ ☠ ☠

David Hughes, an old, retired army colonel I know, rode a yak through the Himalayas while installing an Internet hookup at the base of Everest, at the age of seventy. If I didn't already think he was nuts, this sealed it. He is far, far more daring than I will ever be.

❏ 156. Ride a mechanical bull.
☠ ☠ ☠

You don't see these around much anymore. There's a reason for that. This has all the appeal of riding a real bull outdoors, with the added fun of being able to collide with a wall, the ceiling, drunken onlookers wearing big belt buckles, some tables, various glass objects, and a floor that's much harder than a pasture.

❏ 157. Drive a dogsled.
☠ ☠

It's a sled, in the snow, pulled by a pack of dogs. Balance counts.

158. Race a dogsled.

☠ ☠ ☠

It's a bunch of dogsleds, all trying to beat each other to the finish line. The mass start is the most fascinating aspect of this race, as the dogs would much rather meet the other dogs, run around, jump, play—pretty much do anything other than drag your sorry ass toward the finish line.

159. Enter the Iditarod.

☠ ☠ ☠ ☠

This is a dogsled race across Alaska. Alaska is a big state. It is also cold. This is a good way to kill dogs. Granted, there seem to be rules against "abusing" the animals, but making a dog drag you nonstop across 1,100 miles seems pretty much like the definition of abuse, at least to me.

160. Ride a skateboard.

☠ ☠

Jump it over something. In front of people. Wipe out. This is expressly created for fourteen-year-olds.

161. Enter a skateboard competition.

☠ ☠ ☠ ☠

There are actually several skateboard-related events in the popular X Games. These include Big Air, Street, and Vert.

162. Ride a bicycle.

☠

Yes, you can fall off. But millions of people worldwide do this all the time—how difficult can it really be? Get rid of the training wheels as soon as you can; they make you lose major cool points.

163. Ride a BMX bike.

☠ ☠

It stands for "bicycle motocross," in case you were wondering. Usually a small, sturdy, lightweight frame, with heavy, ridged tires, for purposes of going off-road and doing tricks. People over the age of thirty need not apply.

164. Participate in a BMX race.

☠ ☠ ☠

There are all sorts of jumps and obstacles and turns, all on an unpaved course. This is a good way to learn to eat dirt.

165. Take employment as a bike messenger in a metropolitan area.

☠ ☠ ☠ ☠

Potholes. Traffic. Pedestrians. Curbs. Many, many ways to die. And speed is your trade. Good luck.

166. Ride a bicycle across the United States.

☠ ☠ ☠ ☠ ☠

Just think of the valuable exercise this will afford you! Think of the grandeur of the scenery! Think of the complete and utter exhaustion you will face each night.

❏ 167. Ride a unicycle.

I think you have to be part clown to do this. This necessitates a ludicrous degree of balance and timing, and you look silly doing it. But—what a conversation starter, eh? If you can do this and juggle at the same time, you have a career waiting.

❏ 168. Walk on crutches.

Sort of the same thing. You need less balance for the crutches, though. Although the unicycle doesn't chafe your armpits nearly as much. . . .

❏ 169. Do a triathlon.

This was one of those "sports" invented by those who didn't find one particular event enough of a challenge. A race comprised of one leg of swimming, one of biking, and a run (usually in that order), this is pure punishment. The participant must go from one phase to the next, while the time in transit is counted right along with the time of each event.

❏ 170. Do an "adventure race."

A grueling, lengthy, nonstop race that involves a host of daring activities, such as open-field orienteering (navigation), running, biking, climbing, rafting, etc., etc. Pure zaniness. I guess if they gave out prizes, like a new car or something, just for completing one of these, I'd consider it.

171. Swim with dolphins.

☠☠

Awww . . . aren't they cute? Don't you just love those funny little clicking-whistling noises they make? They're just so sweet on TV and in the movies, aren't they? They're wild animals. Get over it. They're not there for your amusement, and they don't like you. There are plenty of places that will prostitute these animals, though; you can find them all over the Caribbean, the Mexican Riviera, Hawaii, and Florida.

172. Swim with manta rays/skates.

☠☠

So I'm underwater, scuba-equipped and such, just tooling around below the surface of the ocean. And then there's this big, dark shape about twenty feet away. Now, I know mantas aren't vicious; I know they don't normally attack people. But they're really big. And they're awfully scary looking. I'm not even done being scared when it decides it's done looking at me, and it *pumps* its wings once, twice, and it is gone. I'm watching it fly away, at some speed I can't even estimate, and I'm left thinking I got to see one of the coolest wild animals I've ever seen.

173. Swim with jellyfish.

☠☠ ☠☠ ☠☠

Sure, we all know they sting, and that their sting hurts in a nasty, severe way. But did you know they swarm? The evil little bastards can get together in clusters of hundreds, all just floating serenely, doing whatever the hell it is that jellyfish do, waiting for some unwary swimmer to hit them and get stung repeatedly. Ugly.

PART 1 PUBLIC THINGS

49

□ 174. Swim with sharks.

☠ ☠ ☠ ☠ ☠

The shark is nature's perfect critter: Millions of years of evolution have not changed this animal; it is perfectly suited to hunt and kill in its environment. According to the Florida Museum of Natural History's International Shark Attack File, the number of shark attacks is steadily increasing each decade. According to the file, though, this is only because of an increase in the number of people getting close to sharks. Not that this will comfort you in any way if you end up with a three-tiered chomp on your abdomen.

□ 175. Observe whales from a boat smaller than the whales.

☠ ☠ ☠

Yeah, we've heard all the goopy stories from those geeks that go out on Alaskan cruises in the hopes of some spiritual connection with a silly seagoing mammal. And those people are definitely far too saccharine to be wholly believed. But I will say this: When you realize that shadow under the boat is a living thing, with a mind of its own, which could very easily obliterate the craft and all aboard, that is powerful.

□ 176. Swim with whales.

☠ ☠ ☠ ☠

Okay, they're majestic and cool and big and stuff. Seeing them from the boat is an awe-inspiring experience. Now, why would you push your luck and actually take the chance of annoying one of them? Crazy.

❏ 177. Learn to scuba-dive.
☠ ☠

It's not easy to get used to breathing underwater; it's surreal in a very concrete way. You're underwater, and you're breathing. This makes no sense. It takes time to wrap your head around it, and to acclimate your body to the various ways of not dying. But this is as close to freefall as us nonastronauts will get, without the sickening "I'm constantly dropping" sensation. Righteous. Go get information from the international instruction entities before signing up for any scuba school: NAUI (*www.naui.com*) and PADI (*www.padi.com*).

❏ 178. Scuba in an open body of water.
☠ ☠ ☠

Without the sides and bottom of the pool to guide you, diving takes on a whole new promise: the promise of getting lost. Pay attention, stay calm, and remember your training.

❏ 179. Scuba in the ocean.
☠ ☠ ☠ ☠

Go back and check out that entry about bodysurfing. The ocean is even less forgiving to those who are pretending to be at home in it by breathing through an artificial device. Don't be dumb, and you can have a great time.

PART 1 PUBLIC THINGS

51

180. Dive the Great Barrier Reef.

☠ ☠ ☠

This was one of my Ten Things to Do Before I Die. It lived up to my every expectation, and then some. Water the temperature of a comfortable tub, visibility that seems better than above the surface, teeming with wildlife and color—do whatever it takes to do this.

181. Dive Waikiki.

☠ ☠

Yes, it's also a fancy, famous beach—but there's some damned good diving right off the shore. Once the island shelf drops off, it gets wickedly deep, but the water is warm, clear, and full of critters. Very, very cool. Sometimes, it's difficult to remember that this is an American state. Hawaii is a far cry from Nebraska.

182. Scuba in a cave.

☠ ☠ ☠

Known as "cave diving," this combines the thrill of going both underwater and underground. What better way to fulfill your claustrophobia quota for the rest of your natural life? Be sure to bring some light sources; it's doubly dark down there. Water-filled caves can be found all over the world.

183. Scuba in an ice cave.

☠ ☠ ☠ ☠

You get the combined pleasure of knowing you can drown, freeze to death, and get stuck, all at once. Try the Arctic Circle for glacier-mounted ice caves.

❏ 184. Get punched in the face, at least once.

☠ ☠ ☠

We don't let just anyone come close to our face—it is uncomfortable. Up close and personal, you can smell someone's breath, see all the little faults, and there's the constant threat that they will kiss you. So getting punched in the face is a miserable experience; it drops everything you are to a simple common denominator: "I just got punched in the face." Word of warning: A punch in the face causes a lot more damage in real life than in the movies—to both the puncher and the punchee.

❏ 185. Get punched in the gut, at least once.

☠ ☠ ☠

You see someone get punched in the gut, and you don't have nearly as visceral a reaction as when you see someone punched in the face. This is a misleading vestige of our cultural prejudices: Getting punched in the gut hurts a lot worse, and is much more debilitating in the short term. You lose your wind, your body's immediate urge is to double over, and you're left without much energy. A body blow is the roughest.

❏ 186. Get choked-out, at least once.

☠ ☠ ☠ ☠

In judo, this used to be a legal tactic to use on your opponent—as was breaking his or her arm. This has since been restricted a bit, but is still legit in the sport. I was always amazed how long it actually took for someone to be forced into unconsciousness—people can stay awake a pretty long time without air. Or maybe it just seems that way.

❑ 187. Suffer a broken limb, at least once.

☠ ☠ ☠

Go for a simple fracture—those compound fractures are just icky.

❑ 188. Tear a ligament.

☠ ☠ ☠ ☠

These mend less quickly and successfully than bones. You may never get the full use back, and will almost certainly be reminded by the ligament, for the rest of your life, that you once tore it.

❑ 189. Tear some cartilage.

☠ ☠

It's amazing what modern science can do to fix wayward joints nowadays. Totally amazing. I predict that future surgeons will have synthetic cartilage at their disposal.

❑ 190. Learn a martial art.

☠ ☠ ☠

Martial arts, unlike other contact sports, promise the supposition that if you're good, really good, you won't have to get hit. Don't believe it—nobody's that good. Bruce Lee wasn't that good. And you're not Bruce Lee.

❑ 191. Learn a wildly bizarre, difficult, and crazy martial art.

☠ ☠

Give Capoeira a try, for instance. It's a Brazilian thing. You're dancing—no, you're fighting! You're fighting and dancing. Not for the weak-kneed.

192. Fight someone in a competition.
☠ ☠ ☠

You get the great fun of being punched (and kicked) in the head and body, with the additional bonus of getting to be humiliated in front of an audience.

193. Fight someone obviously far more skilled than you.
☠ ☠ ☠

Okay, that punch you see coming, that's the easy one; that one is just going to snap your head backwards, bend your neck a little, give you that sharp slapping pain. The tough one is the one they tell you about when you find yourself on the mat, with no concept of how you got there—you were just upright one instant ago, weren't you? No—you got put down, and you have been lying there for five seconds, your eyes open but unfocused. That's what they call "getting hit on the buzzer."

194. Fight someone much taller than you.
☠ ☠ ☠

This gives your opponent a natural advantage, known as "reach"—the ability, through basic length of limb, to tag you while remaining outside the range of your attacks.

❑ 195. Fight someone much heavier than you.
☠ ☠ ☠

Momentum is a bitch. If your opponent charges you, it's unlikely you're going to be able to halt the onslaught. The best you can do is dodge and try to deliver blows in passing.

❑ 196. Extra added bonus: Fight someone in a completely different style than the one you know.
☠ ☠ ☠ ☠ ☠

Ask any cop where to hit someone with a nightstick, and he or she will explain to you that rapping someone on the shin will put that person on the ground, no matter how big or tough he is. Thai kickboxers know this, which is why they train by brutally slamming their shins (and forearms, and other bony places) against hard surfaces. Think you're Billy Badass? Do not screw with a Thai kickboxer.

❑ 197. Wrestle.
☠ ☠ ☠

Strip down to the bare minimum amount of clothing and protective gear. Face off against another person on a mat; grapple with him, cling to him, try to pin him down.

❑ 198. Box.
☠ ☠ ☠

Unlike many other martial arts/sports, boxing pretty much guarantees that you are going to get punched. When scoring a boxing match, the judge(s) count the number of blows landed by each competitor, per round. The fighter who lands more blows in a given round wins that round. The fighter who wins the most number of rounds wins the match. That's a lot of punches, both being thrown and received.

❒ 199. Try fencing.

Sure, the end of the foil (that stabby thing? that's a foil, or saber, or an épée) is blunted; you can't really poke through anything (like, say, skin) with the tip. Tell that to your eye when it comes whipping past your face. Your reflexes say "go," when you're supposed to be doing something about it . . . like fighting back.

❒ 200. Try walking in snowshoes.

Just for giggles, try running in them. This is a skill that requires a good bit of practice. But don't worry—we're laughing with you.

❒ 201. Play jai alai.

One phrase: "fastest-moving ball in sports." We're talking 180 miles per hour. Sure, it's only a quarter pound, but that's still going to leave a mark. Imagine getting hit by a half-brick thrown from a speeding motorcycle. Which is kinda funny, when you think about it. But not so funny when it's a jai alai pelota hurled by some crazed Basque. Although, it's a lot of fun to say "jai alai" and "pelota." And "Basque."

❑ 202. Try water-skiing.

☠ ☠

This is a special technique, devised by early-twentieth-century Americans, with which to force as much water into your lungs as possible, in the shortest conceivable length of time. Want that lake drained? Hire some water-skiers. If you go face-first into the water, that water is going into your face at the speed the boat was traveling when you hit the surface—and you have holes in your face. The water, as water does, will look for the path of least resistance. That's the holes in your face. Which the water will enter—quickly.

❑ 203. Then try water-skiing on one ski.

☠ ☠ ☠

Some experts claim this is actually easier than with two skis. Don't believe them.

❑ 204. Water-ski barefoot.

☠ ☠ ☠ ☠

This is one of those things you see in James Bond movies. . . . Sure, somewhere there are human beings who can do it, and even do it for fun. However, this basically reduces the glory of human existence into acting like a rather big lure used in fly-fishing.

❑ 205. Try kneeboarding.

☠ ☠

Supposedly easier than other activities in which a person is pulled around a body of water by a motorboat, kneeboarding is just like it sounds: The participant kneels on a plank, balancing, and is then dragged by a boat. I never found it much easier than water-skiing. But I was never that good at water-skiing, either.

☐ 206. Toboggan.
☠ – ☠ ☠, depending on conditions
The advanced form of sledding down a hill. The best of these have actual tracks for the elongated sled to ride on, making the ride a lot more fast (and a lot less dangerous).

☐ 207. Go down the Cresta Run.
☠ ☠ ☠ ☠
A three-quarter-mile run that drops 514 feet, located in St. Moritz, one of only three cities that have twice held the Winter Olympics. Not for the squeamish, as the most popular technique is headfirst. Beginners can give it a whirl for only 500 Swiss francs. Icy-quick peril might be your idea of fun.

☐ 208. Snow tube.
☠
Sledding on an inflated inner tube. Be prepared to flip ass over teakettle, and don't expect to be able to steer. Avoid trees. A load of fun.

☐ 209. River tube.
☠
Same thing. Except on water. You won't hit the hard, hard ground, but you can drown.

PART 1 PUBLIC THINGS

❏ 210. Bobsled.

☠ ☠

I can't believe they give out awards for this; this is sitting in a chair and sliding downhill. I mean, this isn't a function of talent; it's a benefit of gravity. How easy, how fun! You can do this at the old Lake Placid Olympic facility—even in the summer.

❏ 211. Luge.

☠ ☠ ☠ ☠

Start with a bobsled. Take away the camaraderie offered by cramming next to someone of the same gender while wearing polyurethane winter speed suits. Take away the comfort of sitting like a normal human being. Take away the sides and front end of the vehicle. What you're left with is luge.

❏ 212. Street luge.

☠ ☠ ☠ ☠

Laying on your back, on a composite-metal frame, speeding feet-first down a hilly road, your head is propped up so you can look out over your toes at what's coming. You're inches from the concrete. You can—theoretically—steer. In the words of my friend Andrew Harley: "There's a game definitely invented when Mom wasn't home." It started in Southern California, of course. It's now worldwide, with competitions on this continent, Europe, and Africa.

❏ 213. Play Murderball.

☠ ☠ ☠ ☠

Also known as "quad rugby" and "wheelchair rugby," this is a game involving wheelchairs, a ball, and a bunch of guys that try to beat the snot out of each other. Okay, the major problem with this Thing is that you have to be a quadriplegic to participate . . . and damned tough, too. Of course, if you ask nice, they might let you try it, just for fun. If you do, you've got more guts than I do.

☐ 214. Play Hornussen.
☠ ☠ ☠

Supposedly, this Swiss sport involves a projectile moving at speeds above 150 miles per hour. A bizarre combination of golf and tennis, hornussen involves two competing teams that try to block each other's missiles, which are launched with a whiplike club. The further your "nouss" (the pucklike projectile) travels, the more points you get . . . but your opponents are allowed to knock it down mid-flight, using big paddles that look like signs you'd see protesters carrying. Bizarre. Oh—and you have to go to Switzerland to play.

☐ 215. Go hang-gliding off a cliff.
☠ ☠ ☠ ☠

Now that we, as a race, have finally accomplished the goal of creating a mechanism whereby we can take to the air, traversing the atmosphere, in a safe, reliable manner, why not go for it? Do you think it would be a good idea to tie yourself to a kite and jump off something—high? A hang glider is a fabric wing, with straps (or a chassis, depending on the type) to secure the human pilot below it. The pilot steers either by shifting body weight or by using controls on the wing itself (again, depending on the type of hang glider).

216. Go parasailing.

☠

Take the driving force of water-skiing, add to it the dubious merits of skydiving, and you have this contraption. You are now a tethered feather, dragged along above the water.

217. Try paragliding.

☠ ☠ ☠

This is not parasailing. Parasailing has you tethered to a motorboat, like a ridiculous human kite. Paragliding, on the other hand, is a means of actually propelling yourself through the sky, using only a running start, the wind currents, and aeronautics to move you, like a ridiculous human kite. It's very similar to hang-gliding, except that the wing is comprised of a series of fabric cells, instead of a rigid wing. You may want to get a little training before you try something like this.

218. Try paramotoring (powered paragliding).

☠ ☠ ☠ ☠ ☠

As if paragliding isn't insane enough—try paragliding with a propeller strapped to your ass, pushing you through the sky. That's paramotoring.

219. Try spelunking.

☠ ☠ ☠ – ☠ ☠ ☠ ☠ ☠, depending on whether or not you suffer from acrophobia/claustrophobia

There's a big hole in the ground. . . . Wanna go down into it? It'll be really dark, and we'll have to use all the skills, techniques, and equipment utilized in mountain climbing. Won't that be fun? Doubly so, if you're acrophobic and claustrophobic.

☐ 220. Launch an arrow using a bow.
☠ ☠

A big, honking compound bow. Feel that sharp, slapping sting on your forearm? That's 'cause you didn't bend your elbow enough. The bow is probably the only self-correcting weapon that isn't fatal.

☐ 221. Hunt an animal with a bow.
☠ ☠ – ☠ ☠ ☠ ☠ ☠, depending on prey

Going after game with a rifled weapon, giving you the ability to zap your prey from a football field's distance, seems none too daring to me. Hunting with a bow, however, is pretty damned intense. Even getting close to tag a critter is an accomplishment. For a really gutsy Thing, try something that has the capacity to kick your ass in return, like a moose or bear.

☐ 222. Fire a bolt using a crossbow.
☠

All of the benefits of a bow, with none of the drawbacks. So simple, even a child can put a projectile through the wall of a house. These can be cocked with a lever mechanism, making them easier to draw, and are fired by pulling a trigger, making it possible to hold your aim indefinitely. Also, it's aimed like longarm, with the bow horizontal, allowing an easier line of sight, and good placement for a scope.

❑ 223. Do a William Tell impersonation.

☠ ☠ ☠ ☠ ☠

This would entail using your crossbow to shoot a piece of fruit off the head of a child. It's probably illegal in most states. Not to mention stupid.

❑ 224. Pilot a kayak.

☠ ☠ ☠

So canoeing is too easy, you say? Rafting just doesn't have that thrill of a rugged individual sport? Try kayaking. You're right-side up—then you're upside down. You're fighting a body of water of some kind, and you're all on your own.

❑ 225. Pilot a kayak through some rapids.

☠ ☠ ☠ ☠

Remember, you want to breathe when your head is above the surface. It's easier that way.

❑ 226. Pilot a sea kayak.

☠ ☠

This is a kayak specifically designed for large, open bodies of water, like lakes, bays, seas, and oceans. Less maneuverable than its river-borne counterpart, the sea kayak offers cargo space instead. You can take a trip lasting several days in one of these, carrying everything you might possibly need.

1001 THINGS TO DO IF YOU DARE

☐ 227. Sail a small (less than three-person) sailboat.

☠ ☠

There are all sorts of hooks and pulleys and big pieces of cloth, and you have to make them all work together. If you can pull this off, you are able to replicate one of the oldest forms of locomotion in human history, traveling the way our distant ancestors did. Why you'd want to, when cigarette boats are available, is beyond me.

☐ 228. Sail a yacht.

☠ ☠ ☠

One of those big mothers. On the open ocean. Look out for pirates and sea monsters and stuff.

☐ 229. Go on a cruise.

☠

Yeah, maybe it's pretty simple, but there are still pirates, tidal waves, and various possible malfunctions that could sink the boat. Which are just a few of the reasons I've never done this.

☐ 230. Go land-sailing.

☠ ☠

A small-wheeled craft, propelled by wind, using a sail, that traverses land. Because . . . a car just wasn't good enough? Who knows?

❏ 231. Try Parkour.

☠

Yeah, it's stupid. It's also French. You run around in the streets, jumping and climbing over stuff. We did this when we were kids (although we never called it "Parkour"). We were stupid. At least we weren't French. A guy named David Belle invented it, allegedly to satisfy his jones for martial arts movies and running around.

❏ 232. Wrestle an alligator.

☠ ☠ ☠ ☠ ☠

Here's a giant reptile, about as unevolved as a shark (no need to evolve when you're an almost perfectly designed predator). Isn't it a cool giant reptile? Let's grab it and fight with it, mano a mano. Because, you know, we're equipped with these wicked fingernails and massive muscles. . . . Oh, wait. There are plenty of places in Florida (and nearby states) where you can go see this—but none that will let you, the tourist, try it. The liability is just too great.

❏ 233. Wrestle a bear.

☠ ☠ ☠ ☠ ☠

Here's the most formidable, omnivorous mammal in the world. According to several news sources, bear wrestling is illegal in twenty states. Before attempting, find out if it's permissible in your locale. If it is, still avoid this.

234. Attempt extreme ironing.
☠ ☠ ☠ ☠

From the Web site of the Extreme Ironing Bureau (*www.extreme ironing.com*): "The sport that is 'extreme ironing' is an outdoor activity that combines the danger and excitement of an 'extreme' sport with the satisfaction of a well pressed shirt." Ironers have ironed on top of mountains, under bogs, and on nude beaches. Because, even when you're doing something extremely danger- ous, it's important to be well-pressed. Supposedly, there's some dude ironing underwater in Madagascar. Righteous.

235. Participate in a rodeo.
☠ ☠ ☠ ☠

This is an activity that involves kicking farm critters with metal spikes worn on your heels, in order to infuriate them. Now, I'm not a bronco or a bull or anything, but I guarantee you, if you ever jumped on my back, jabbed spurs into my side, and tried to make me do something, I'd be pretty pissed off, too.

236. Attempt bull riding.
☠ ☠ ☠ ☠

A rodeo event wherein you, the rider, get on a large male bovine and try to remain there for eight seconds, holding on with only one hand. This could have quite easily been started as a cowboy- fraternity initiation prank.

237. Go bronc riding.
☠ ☠ ☠ ☠

That's short for "bronco," as in "wild horse." Like in bull riding, this rodeo event requires the human rider to remain on the animal for eight seconds, using only one hand. This is done both with and without saddles, and the distinct events are known as "saddle bronc riding" and "bareback bronc riding," in creative fashion.

☐ 238. Try steer wrestling.

☠☠ ☠☠ ☠☠

More rodeo fun. A castrated bull is loosed from a pen into an arena. A cowboy rides after it on a horse. The cowboy jumps off the horse, grabs the steer, and wrestles it to the ground. Yee. Haw.

☐ 239. Do some team roping.

☠☠ ☠☠ ☠☠

Another rodeo event, this time involving a pair of riders who try to rope a steer. The first rider has to lasso the horns of the animal, and the second has to get the rear hooves. Agility and timing are essential.

☐ 240. Conduct calf roping.

☠☠ ☠☠

A rider lassos a young cow. The competitor then throws the animal to the ground and ties three of its legs together. The event is scored on speed.

241. Steer roping.
☠ ☠

Like calf roping, but with a steer. Of course, the participant does not have to throw the steer to the ground.

242. Try barrel racing.
☠ ☠

No, you don't have to race a barrel. You have to ride a horse around a series of barrels, as quickly as possible. The rider may touch—but not knock over—the barrels. And if you lose your cowboy hat during the event, you must pay a fine. No kidding.

243. Engage in breakaway roping.
☠ ☠

Much like the calf roping and steer roping events, this involves a rider throwing a rope around the horns of a runaway calf. This event ends when the easily broken string at the end of the rope snaps, signaling that the rope was tied securely between the calf and the pommel on the saddle of the rider's horse.

244. Try goat tying.
☠ ☠

In an arena, you ride a horse, very quickly, to the opposite end of the arena, where a goat is tied up. You jump off the horse, grab the goat, throw it on the ground, and tie three of its legs. I wonder why.

PART 1 PUBLIC THINGS

❏ 245. Go pole bending.
☠ ☠

Similar to barrel racing, the competitor slaloms through a line of poles, while on horseback. I am forced to wonder what the horse may think of this activity. Probably something like, "Mmm-mmm . . . Oats."

❏ 246. Fight a bull.
☠ ☠ ☠ ☠

Sword? Check. Cape? Check. Shiny pants? Check. Okay, you're now well armed to go up against a ton of vicious animal flesh. But in the traditional form, you can't just go do that—no, you have to get eight of your friends to poke and harass the poor creature first, and weaken it to the point where you really don't have to do much work yourself. I root for the bull.

❏ 247. Learn to use nunchaku.
☠

A decorative weapon made of two lengths of wood/plastic/metal, connected by a chain or rope. Wielding this weapon looks a lot harder than it really is; it's really just an exercise in timing and concentration. Lots of concentration. So when you're starting out, and you're practicing that pass between your legs, turn off the telephone ringer. Trust me.

❏ 248. Learn to use two nunchaku simultaneously.
☠ ☠

One in each hand. Not as complicated as it looks, but not really very useful for anything, either.

249. Do a logroll.

☠ ☠

Supposedly, this comes from the dated practice of sending logs downriver to the sawmill. The lumberjacks had to ride the logs on the water, to assist in preventing logjams. (See the Paul Newman movie *Sometimes a Great Notion*, based on the excellent book by Ken Kesey, if you can find a copy.) You're standing on a log, which is floating in the water. There is also an opponent standing on the log. You both try to spin the log as it floats, with the objective of getting the other person to fall. This could have an adverse effect on your sex life.

250. Enter the Highland Games.

☠ ☠

There are a set of rudimentary activities involved in this, but mainly it is comprised of throwing a variety of inanimate objects, such as a pole, a sheaf of straw, a rock, and a hammer. Nobody is sure why the Scots are so big on throwing things; the origins of these events are mostly lost in time, and shrouded in legend and mystery.

251. Go fishing.

☠

Not the most dramatic of Things, fishing can be done while basically sitting on your ass next to a body of water, or even napping. You throw a line with a hook and some bait into the water, and wait for the fish to snag itself. Possibly the most passive form of gathering food.

□ 252. Try fly-fishing.

☠ ☠

This requires a different kind of pole-and-reel setup, one designed to make this activity somewhat more participatory than normal fishing. You try to snap the end of your line right on top of the water, like an extremely tiny bullwhip, mimicking the behavior of an insect, and hope the fish fall for the trick. They probably will: fish are pretty stupid.

□ 253. Go deep-sea fishing.

☠

A macho goofball author once wrote a book all about an old guy who went and did this, and had a rotten time. I kind of think that's fairly accurate. You: sit in a boat, in a comfy chair, with as many beers as you'd like, and a high-tech rod and reel designed specifically to yank game fish out of the ocean. The fish: gets snagged in the mouth by a hook and fights for its life. Gosh, you're impressive. Hang that thing on your wall.

□ 254. Try your hand at commercial fishing.

☠ ☠ ☠ ☠ ☠

There are heavy ropes, cold seas, harsh conditions, giant storms, pirates, and big-ass fish ready to knock you overboard into turbulent water. Let's hope there's good money in it, because, according to the federal Centers for Disease Control (which tracks stuff like this), Alaskan commercial fishing resulted in 28 times more occupational deaths than the U.S. average, as of the turn of the twenty-first century. National average: 4.4 deaths per 100,000 workers each year; Alaskan commercial fishers: 124 deaths per 100,000 workers.

☐ 255. Go spearfishing.
☠ ☠ ☠

A lot more complicated than regular fishing: this is just you, a pointy stick, and the free-roaming fish (well, as free-roaming as fish get—they gotta stay in the water, of course). You have to be able to nail a moving creature, taking into account the diffraction of reflected light from water to air, just by jabbing quickly. Tough.

☐ 256. Go spearfishing while diving.
☠ ☠

You can do this with or without scuba tanks, but it's more challenging without them—this is the fish's element, not yours. The spear gun brings you some parity, though. You can nail trophy fish, and—theoretically—game fish; then you stuff them into a mesh bag to carry them back to the shore/boat. Remember: you've got a bloody fish attached to your hip, and sharks can smell blood.

☐ 257. Tickle a fish.
☠ ☠

No, you ain't trying to make the fish laugh. *Tickling* is the term used to describe the practice of grabbing a fish with your bare hands. Really. Evidently, it can actually be accomplished. Which is pretty damned impressive, if you ask me. Be careful, though—

while the fish-tickling season in Kentucky lasts from the first of June through the end of August, the activity is prohibited altogether in Kansas.

❏ 258. Fish with explosives.

☠ ☠ ☠ ☠

I've never done this, because it seems ten kinds of dumb to me. Jack London's story "Moon-Face" mentions it. Supposedly, it's still done in a lot of Third-World countries. Also known as "blast fishing," this involves throwing some sort of explosive into the water; the concussion and shock wave kill everything within a given distance—everything. Not cool, and very illegal in the United States. This is especially harmful to coral reefs.

❏ 259. Go ice-fishing.

☠ ☠ ☠

Find a body of water that has frozen over (one that has fish in it, preferably). Cut a hole in the ice so that you have access to the wet stuff underneath. Drop your fishing line down into the water. Sit and wait until you catch a fish. I think this is really mostly about drinking beer.

❏ 260. Go crabbing.

☠ ☠ ☠

Trying to harvest crabs is not a simple, sedentary pursuit, like some other types of fishing. Crabs are scuttling, frisky things, with pincers designed to, well, pinch. They will let you know that they don't like being harvested in the manner best suited to their species. Most crabbing is done via the use of traps;

cagelike boxes of metal or wood, which allow the crabs to walk right in and sample whatever bait you've placed inside. You drop your trap down into the water, letting it sink to the bottom. A buoy attached to a line on the trap lets you know where you left it. You go back after a while and pull the thing back up. Maybe there's crabs inside, maybe there aren't. Check all local laws before attempting—different places have widely varying rules.

❏ 261. Bring in the lobsters.

☠ ☠ ☠ ☠

To catch lobsters, like crabs, you set traps. These are often wire mesh nets, in a sophisticated shape, such that the lobster can get in but not out. You can also try to catch lobsters by hand, while diving. Lobsters don't want to be caught—and the Northern ones have big claws. Bear that in mind. Lobsters only exist in saltwater.

❏ 262. Try pole sitting.

☠ ☠ ☠

Climb atop a high structure. Perch on a small pedestal set on a pole. Do that for a while. For some reason, this was popular back in the 1920s. Hey, maybe you can jump-start a revival!

❏ 263. Learn to throw a bladed tool of some kind.

☠

There are plenty of things designed specifically for throwing, and many of them are pointed or edged. There are special throwing knives, throwing axes, and the ever-popular "throwing stars," or shuriken, from martial arts movies. They are also pretty simple to use, if you've got some patience. You can set up a training area anywhere you want: your bedroom, the basement, outside. Anywhere with enough distance to throw something accurately (say, ten yards, tops). Make sure you have a good backstop so that you're not throwing sharp things past your target; a nice, wide, wooden tabletop, hefted vertically, is a good choice. And try not to scare the neighbors.

❏ 264. Let someone throw a bladed tool of some kind at you.

☠ ☠ ☠ ☠

Oh, good idea. Sure—they're an expert. According to them, any-way. The number of possible things that might go wrong, and the sheer volume of things that could happen because of them, stagger the imagination.

❏ 265. Throw a spear/javelin.

☠ ☠

It looks as if it would be easy, because gravity's doing most of the work, right? Actually hitting something you're aiming at, or even getting a considerable distance, though, is a bit more tricky. You need a nice, long, empty area to practice this, the size of a public park or playing field—but both those places discourage people from throwing pointy objects up in the air, because the pointy objects have to come down sometime. Which seems reasonable.

❒ 266. Swing on a trapeze.

☠ ☠

Maybe it's corny, but it's also a lot of fun. It's like the grown-up version of the swing set. Hopefully, unlike the swing set, you have a safety net beneath you.

❒ 267. Swing on a giant swing.

☠ ☠

This is a cross between a bungee jump and the aforementioned swing set. Often, each ride is shared by three passengers, from heights that top 180 feet, resulting in an arc that's . . . well . . . huge. Sometimes billed under different names, depending on the vendor selling rides. I found one at the MGM casino in Las Vegas, but it's not there anymore. Keep an eye out at traveling carnivals, theme parks, and the like.

❒ 268. Walk on stilts.

☠ ☠

It's spooky, teetering up so high, with nothing to support you but your own treasonous sense of balance. But if you have the patience to learn this, just think: you can always make a practice of scaring small children by being that person who dresses up for the parade and ambles along, staring down at people and waving.

❒ 269. Jump on a trampoline.

☠

Try some flips and somersaults and stuff. Go for the gusto. If you're over the age of 25, you'll be amazed how quickly your leg muscles succumb to a burning sensation. And how much it hurts when you fall.

❏ 270. Throw a bolas.

☠ ☠ ☠

Here's a dandy little tool that can quite easily kill the wielder just as readily as function properly. Made of strips of leather or rope with heavy weights on the end, the bolas is used primarily in South America to trip large animals. It's thrown by gauchos. So, if nothing else comes of the experience, you get to use the word *gaucho* quite often, which is a big bonus. You might not want to try this when you're having an "off" day. For target practice, you'll want to find something upright and fairly narrow, like a young tree or fencepost. These aren't too good over long distances, though—stay within twenty yards.

❏ 271. Crack a bullwhip.

☠ ☠ ☠ ☠

It's really not as hard to crack a bullwhip as you might think. Of course, controlling where the thing cracks, and what it does before and after the crack, is something else entirely. And that nifty stuff they do with whips, in movies? Like having the whip twist around a beam so that the wielder can swing from one place to another, or grab a person's limb, or whatever? Not real likely.

272. Ride a pogo stick.

☠

You go up. You go down. Repeatedly and quickly. Bouncy-bounce. How long can you stay up? Long enough to make yourself nauseous?

273. Swing on a rope from one place to another.

☠ ☠

Of course, it is traditional to give full voice to a Tarzan-like yodel as you're traversing space. For which you receive style points. You may have to set this up on your own property, with the rope attached to a house or tree.

274. Roll down a hill.

☠

If you've never done this, you may as well consider your entire childhood a wasted effort. Sure, you get so dizzy you might barf, but that's part of the thrill, if I remember correctly.

275. Roll down a hill in a Zorb.

☠

Ever have a hamster? Okay, ever see a hamster? You know those little plastic balls they roll around in? Well, now somebody makes giant ones, suitable for people, surrounded by soft plastic air cushions. So if you've ever wanted to be a hamster, or just feel like a hamster, this is the thing for you. For inspiration, you can watch reruns of *The Prisoner*.

❏ 276. River-bugging.

☠ ☠

Okay, this is pretty spiffy. Basically, it's an inflatable easychair that supports your butt and back, but lets your legs dangle. You then throw it (and yourself) into a river and scoot downstream. Having your legs available gives you the ability to spring around and over obstacles like, well, water bugs. Hence the name.

❏ 277. Hunt a falcon.

☠ ☠ ☠

No, I don't mean go out with a shotgun and stalk a bird of prey; I mean you should try being a falconer. Getting a recalcitrant, obstinate, independent animal like a raptor to do your bidding is quite a challenge—and don't romanticize the activity; the birds, while graceful and cool to look at, are smelly, mean, filthy, and damned dangerous. Plus, cutting up various rodents and game birds to feed the hunters is a nasty, unpleasant business.

❏ 278. Fire a handgun.

☠ ☠

What most folks won't tell you, whether they're antigun or not, is that a pistol feels good in your hand. It was designed specifically to fit in your palm and be squeezed. Shooting at something and hitting it, well, that feels fantastic. Try shooting solid targets—bottles and cans. There is something far more satisfying about making something jump or shatter, as opposed to putting tiny little holes in a piece of paper. Be sure you have plenty of room for this—a certified shooting range is best. Know the parameters of your gun and ammo.

☐ 279. Shoot holes in a photo of a former flame.
☠ ☠

There is something grotesquely cathartic about this, much more so than punching a wall or swearing loudly or any of a thousand other means to vent your displeasure. Holes. In a picture. Good.

☐ 280. Fire a rifle.
☠ ☠

This is a lot trickier than a handgun. A rifle is supposed to fit snugly in your arms. It should rest comfortably perched in the crook of your shoulder. Human bodies, however, vary a lot more, and in wildly more ways, than human hands; unless you have a firearm custom-tailored to your body specifications, it's never going to feel as simply correct as a pistol. It's a lot more accurate, though. Rifle rounds travel a long way—longer than you might initially think. A simple .22 can traverse a mile over land, and two miles over water (yes, they can skip). Make sure you have enough open area, or a great backstop.

☐ 281. Fire a sniper rifle.
☠ ☠ ☠

Try to hit something very far away. There are a variety of types and kinds, ranging from the teeny-tiny assassination models, to the massive .50-caliber monsters used to destroy unexploded ordnance. Use a good scope, take a lesson or two, and learn how to hit something almost a mile out. Make sure you're in a place where you're not going to hurt someone, like a range specifically designed for this kind of activity.

☐ 282. Fire a shotgun.

☠ ☠

Most nonshooters have a bizarrely mistaken view of what a shotgun blast is like. This is true for both the kick against your body and the spray of shot that bursts forth. The kick is sizable, and can even hurt, depending on the load you're using. The spray is not nearly as wide as movies make it out to be, and doesn't have great penetrating force over any kind of distance.

☐ 283. Fire a shotgun packing a Magnum, solid-slug load.

☠ ☠ ☠

Makes the normal recoil seem like a soft caress.

☐ 284. Fire a shotgun at trap clays.

☠ ☠ ☠

This activity was supposedly designed to simulate the experience of hunting game birds. Instead of birds, the participant fires a series of quick shotgun blasts at small, round, clay targets. There's a single launching point (a "house") that throws the small disks out ahead of the shooter's position, at varying angles and trajectories. Many people think that a shotgun is some magic destructive paintbrush that will destroy anything in the general vicinity of where it's pointing when fired. Not so—the shot pattern of a group of pellets is actually fairly small—and hitting a fist-sized target flying away from you at a good clip is not nearly as easy as you might think. And be careful selecting your fellow participants; no need to get Cheneyed.

❏ 285. Fire a shotgun at skeet clays.
☠ ☠ ☠

Quite a bit like trap, except that there are multiple "houses," and clays cross the shooter's field of vision instead of launching straight out. To add to the madness, the shooter is required to move to far more shooting positions than with trap. There's actually a kind of pattern of positions, like a perverted baseball diamond, but it's quite baffling. A lot of fun, but frustrating.

❏ 286. Fire a shotgun at sporting clays.
☠ ☠ ☠ ☠

The participants in this activity move to a variety of stations around the course, which can cover much more geographic area than even a skeet field, and are required to shoot at targets flung in a random myriad of ways: away, toward, or across the shooter's field of vision, at differing angles and velocities. No one round of sporting clays is quite like another.

❏ 287. Use a firearm to hunt an animal.
☠

Can't really see the "sport" here. I mean, maybe if you were hunting Kevlar animals and had to hit them in the eye or something, that would be tricky. Going out in the woods to shoot a large mammal, though? Doesn't seem all that tough. Sounds more like an extended, annoying form of golf, but involving more bloody entrails. Not my bag, but some folks swear by it.

☐ 288. Use a firearm to hunt birds.

☠ ☠

You might see how this would be slightly more fun than popping deer—and more challenging, too. It's got more to do with how well you train your hunting dogs than your finesse with a gun, though. And dogs are cool.

☐ 289. Fire an automatic weapon, on automatic.

☠ ☠

Movies and television have led the casual viewer to believe that this technique is an easy way of obliterating whatever you want to destroy. Not so. It's almost impossible to aim a weapon on full auto; the muzzle tends to rise and drift as the repetitive blow-back hammers at your grip. But man—what a rush.

☐ 290. Fire a heavy machine gun.

☠ ☠ ☠

You can only really rock 'n' roll with the Big Bad Mothers: the .50-cal or the M-60, something that throws enough lead to blind Superman. Of course, you're hard-pressed to find that kind of firepower outside the military, but if you can, by all means make the most of it.

☐ 291. Try street-skiing.

☠ ☠ ☠ ☠ ☠

You're on skates, or maybe a skateboard. You hang out at the curb, waiting for a likely vehicle to come by—you grab it, and you're zipping off down the street, towed by an unlikely land yacht. You are seconds away from Scar City.

❏ 292. Play racquetball.

☠ ☠

It's all about speed, motion, and angles. You have to have some serious stamina for this, and a knowledge of rudimentary physics. That ball is small, hard, and made of rubber, and stings if it hits you. Head shots are bad, but exposed skin is even worse—the welts can remain for weeks.

❏ 293. Play racquetball without goggles.

☠ ☠ ☠ ☠

I've only done this a few times, because it's stupidly dangerous. A leading cause of blindness in America, according to the American Academy of Ophthalmology.

❏ 294. Play squash.

☠ ☠ ☠

Another, lamer version of racquetball, with a long, skinny racket and a tiny, harder ball, and a panel that limits the playing area of the front wall.

❏ 295. Skip rope.

☠ ☠ ☠

Oh, yeah—you think it looks easy, right? Think maybe it's a pastime for little kids? So go on, show us what you've got. This takes not just agility and timing, but stamina, too. Why do you think so

PART 1 PUBLIC THINGS

many boxers do this? That's right. If you think it's still too simple, try the arms-crossed stroke, or try doing it with ankle weights.

☐ 296. Ice skate.

A lot like roller-skating, but with sharp, heavy blades strapped to your feet. Depending on whom you ask, ice-skating was invented between 1,200 and 2,000 years ago, initially as a form of transportation, but then became a form of recreation. Requires ankle strength.

☐ 297. Ice-skate on a natural body of water.

You have to wait until it's frozen, of course. And you'd better make sure it's really, really frozen. Few things are worse than getting trapped under the ice in freezing water. According to the Minnesota Department of Natural Resources, that state alone has lost six to seven people per year to "ice-related drownings" over the last quarter-century.

☐ 298. Play hockey.

Ice is not a natural supporter of human life. It saps the strength and energy of wimpy warm-blooded bodies with no fur. So somebody had the bright idea to put a semicontact game on top of the stuff. Go figure.

299. Throw a boomerang.

☠ ☠

Theoretically, if you do it correctly, it will come back to you. Why you'd want a heavy, thin piece of hardwood flying at your body is another story.

GROUP THINGS

There are some athletic activities that simply require more than one person to participate, or at least that's the prerequisite for having fun. This adds another layer to the challenge of the event itself: you now face the additional risk of contributing to the failure of your group, compounding the number of people who might become disgruntled.

300. Raft a white-water river.

☠ – ☠ ☠ ☠ ☠, depending on conditions

You go up and down, side to side, splashing, flailing, twisting, and turning. This is a fantastic experience—and one with the peril of possibly drowning.

301. Raft the Arkansas River, in Colorado.

☠ ☠ – ☠ ☠ ☠ ☠ ☠, depending on conditions

Why is the Arkansas River in Colorado, and the Colorado River in Nevada?

□ 302. Go canoeing for an entire week, out of
touch with civilization, using only the supplies you bring with you and what you can
harvest.

☠ ☠ ☠

There was this old TV show about a guy named Grizzly Adams,
who was a mélange of traditional American mountain man and
crunchy '70s hippie. He lived off the land. He rocked. Go pretend
to be him—it's a rush.

□ 303. Do the canoeing-for-a-week thing, using
only the supplies you bring, in the Upper Man-
itou stretch of the Canadian wilderness.

☠ ☠ ☠

This is an excellent place to go canoeing, with long stretches of
nice water, low cliffs, plenty of wildlife, and short portages.

□ 304. Run with a herd of bulls.

☠ ☠ ☠

You see that bull? Yeah, that one. Doesn't look real fast, does
it? Doesn't seem like it's anything other than a male cow, right?
Just lying there, chewing on some grass, it looks pretty sedentary. Oh—didn't they mention? Bulls can hit running speeds
close to that of a horse—right around 45 miles per hour. The
fastest Olympic runner can do 10.2 meters per second, which
equals roughly 27 miles per hour. So, uh . . . what were you
thinking? This is one of those really stupid things you only do so
you can say you did it. I did it.

305. Play football.

☠ – ☠ ☠ ☠ ☠ ☠, depending on conditions

There are many varieties of this game, from fun-with-the-fam-on-the-lawn-two-hand-touch, to Corporate Grudge Flag, to the ol' fashioned, brain-rattling tackle.

306. Play rugby.

☠ ☠ ☠

I played this game in college, for a whole semester of intramurals. I still have no idea what the hell the rules are. It seems to be a version of combative group hug.

307. Try to pole vault.

☠ ☠ ☠

Physics plays a significant role in this activity. Work on your upper-body strength, and get a damned good coach before attempting this. Really.

308. Play water polo.

☠ ☠

This is like hockey, but actually in the water. So now you can add drowning to the possible implications. Nifty.

309. Play underwater hockey.

☠ ☠ ☠

Okay, now you're under the water. This is quite possibly the most brutal way to punish your lungs and inner ear. The stamina required for this activity outstrips just about everything else. You get a small stick, about two hand-spans long, which you use to push a weighted puck across the bottom of the pool. The opposing team tries to push the puck in the other direction. Fun, but very, very difficult.

❒ 310. Play polo.
☠ ☠ ☠

Hockey on horses. Lots of horses. Really fast horses. And really long mallets. With a big-ass plastic ball that soars at head-height.

❒ 311. Play soccer with Europeans.
☠ ☠ ☠

This is not fun for them. This is not sport. This is religion. Anyone who wasn't sleeping through history class in high school remembers what religious Europeans did when they decided they wanted a chunk of Middle Eastern desert for themselves. Same kind of thing. It will get bloody.

❒ 312. Play slamball.
☠ ☠

Because, y'know, basketball just wasn't intense enough. So they added some trampolines and plastic walls, and took away some of the rules.

❒ 313. Roller-skate.
☠

Some balance is involved. Granted, it's pretty easy once you get the hang of it, but some people never quite accomplish even that.

☐ 314. Play roller derby.

☠ ☠ ☠

You thought this had fled with the 1970s, didn't ya? Well, it did . . . but it keeps trying to spring up again, like a weed. And, admittedly, the fascination is largely attributed to that portion of the brain that also enjoys women-in-prison movies. Two teams of five female players each skate counterclockwise around an oval track. Yes.

☐ 315. Rollerblade.

☠

Like roller-skating, but thinner. And more expensive.

☐ 316. Participate in building a human pyramid.

☠

Well, duh—obviously, it's better to be as close to the top as possible. Of course, then you have farther to fall. . . .

☐ 317. Try sculling.

☠ ☠

Actually, sculling is a subset of the activity entitled "sport rowing," and is the type with two oars (sweep-oar rowing has the participant wielding just one oar). But it's much more fun to say "sculling" than "sport rowing," even though it's much more pretentious. Still, if I had to do this, I'd rather be the coxswain, the person sitting in the front of the boat, yelling at the rowers to row harder.

PART 1 PUBLIC THINGS

91

318. Engage in a hearty round of dodge ball.

☠ ☠ – ☠ ☠ ☠ ☠ ☠, depending on circumstances

Mostly, in this country, dodge ball is played by prepubescent children whose bodies are comprised mostly of spongy cartilage and mucus; it is for this reason that there are so few dodge ball–related permanent injuries and disfigurements in the medical texts. To play as an adult, well, that's bordering on lunacy. Some colleges have formed amateur dodge ball leagues, so if you want to play, you might want to matriculate at Michigan State University, Ohio State, the University of Kentucky, Lesley College, or the Art Institute of Boston. There are rumors of at least one grudge match played between Harvard and MIT. If you're out of college, check out the National Amateur Dodgeball Association, at *www.dodgeballusa.com*.

319. Take part in a cardboard regatta.

☠ ☠

Maybe you find sailing and sculling fun but tame. . . . Why not make your own watercraft out of recyclable paper products? This was someone's nifty idea, and, unfortunately, it never died with that person. So now, supposedly, there are hordes of people across the country who build and propel their own corrugated-cardboard boats. Really.

320. Play paintball.

☠ ☠

There's nothing quite as much fun as shooting your friends. And, while not truly harmful, getting nailed by one of those suckers hurts. Really and truly. So try to remember all the minor slights and insults your friends have caused you over the years, use that for motivation, and get cracking. There are several varieties of games you can play, including versions of "Capture the Flag" and "Tag." Sometimes, though, it's just more fun to re-enact a classical European duel of honor.

☐ 321. Enter a demolition derby.

☠ ☠ ☠

Only in a nation as absurdly oversupplied with technological goodness as our own could such a pastime develop naturally. Here's the deal: a bunch of people take a bunch of cars into an arena. The drivers bash the other people's cars with their own. The last driver with a drivable (moving) car wins. I have heard that it is best to go in reverse during this type of competition, as most vehicles have an engine in the front, and you want to avoid disabling the engine.

SOCIAL THINGS

Let's face it: All our real fears—or most of the serious ones, at any rate—have to do with how we deal with other people. Nothing is as intimidating as our interactions, be they with strangers, friends, family, colleagues, or loved ones. Where do we rank in the eyes of others? How are we supposed to behave? Will we look like idiots, and embarrass ourselves? Even the athletic stuff is compounded by the social aspect—losing a game is bad, but losing it in front of other people, or knowing that other people will hear of the loss, is excruciating.

❒ 322. Walk up to a complete stranger and espouse a viewpoint so utterly ludicrous, so distasteful, nobody could possibly agree with it.

☠

For added excitement, walk up to a group of strangers. For some bizarre reason, and someone should do some scientific research into this phenomenon, you will rarely find anyone who will just curse you outright and tell you to go away.

❒ 323. Take a loud contrary viewpoint in a roomful of people dedicated to the thing you're attacking.

☠ ☠

This is particularly intriguing when it involves politics, religion, or sex. Even more so when includes all three. For instance, you might want to assert that you think Buddha would be against any laws that prohibit sodomy, or that the pope would sanction equal opportunity quotas for prostitutes.

❒ 324. Teach a high school class.

☠ ☠ ☠

Find a teacher in your community who welcomes guest lecturers, preferably on a topic with which you're familiar. Prepare a presentation. Go in and try to make the little monsters learn something. This is the most difficult audience you will ever face: they don't think you're cool, they don't like what you're talking about, and they're only there because the law says they have to be.

❏ 325. Teach a college class.

This is a lot less hassle than the high school variety: college students, by and large, are present because they want to be, on some level. They'll at least give you a modicum of attention and awareness, and might even listen to what you have to say. You can also use curse words and not get in too much trouble.

❏ 326. Teach a class in a subject for which you have no preparation, training, or formal education.

Colloquially called "winging it," this is a test of your ability to think and speak on your feet, and of your store of general information. Like poker, bluffing is a major component. I once spent over an hour talking about typing.

❏ 327. Make a public presentation of some sort. If you're really brave, do it in front of your peers, friends, and relatives.

There are no harsher critics than somebody who knows you intimately—they'll be glad to tell you how much you sucked.

❏ 328. Write a letter to the editor.

Let everybody know what you think. Let them know what you think about a really bizarre topic. This has become less an act

of bravery since the advent of the Internet, where everybody's dumb ideas are exposed to the world at large.

❏ 329. Write a letter of protest.
☠ ☠

Really use your personal freedom, and stand up for what you believe in. Or sit down, rather—it's much easier to write or type while seated. Let someone know how you really feel, and how you think that whatever that person did (or didn't do) was/is wrong. You have to put your actual name on it—anonymous letters of protest are for wimps.

❏ 330. Write a letter of complaint.
☠

A company or person provided you with shoddy service, a bad product, or just out-and-out screwed you. Let them know how you feel. You'd be surprised how far a letter can go toward satisfying you.

❏ 331. Write a letter of compliment.
☠

Someone did you a good turn—let them know that you're appreciative. Better yet, let that person's boss/supervisor/employer know how happy you are.

❏ 332. Take part in a prank that is nothing less than childishly foolish.
☠ ☠

For the sake of argument here, let's say that you make a small mannequin out of an old pair of Levi's and a flannel shirt stuffed with straw, and you pop on a head made from a car-wash sponge mitten. Maybe even pour ketchup over his mitten head, like he's suffered some grievous trauma recently. And then let's just say you prop him out on a suburban road, sitting atop a large hunk of firewood, with his legs crossed, in a graceful manner, like he's drinking a martini and smoking a cigarette. Let's say you do this late on Halloween night. At, like, 11 P.M. or so. You'd obviously hide in the bushes on the side of the road, right? I mean, you'd wait to watch some car drive along and see this dude sitting there, and you'd want to see what they'd do. What would you do if that first car were a squad car?

☐ 333. Run from the cops.
☠ ☠ ☠

Maybe you aren't doing anything bad, per se. Not even really all that illegal. Like maybe underage drinking. And maybe you're just walking along the railroad tracks, headed home. But when you see that cop, the adrenaline kicks in and you bolt for cover.

☐ 334. Get arrested.
☠ ☠ ☠ ☠

Most of the time, our mass media teaches us that cops are to be trusted—that they might have personal foibles, but they're basically good people. Many of our parents, teachers, and other trusted adults tell us this when we're growing up, too. And we learn to assume that cops will be good and trustworthy and fair. When you end up with your hands cuffed behind you, sitting in the back of that squad car, try to remember those things: The experience casts those beliefs into a stark light. Oh, and don't slide your cuffs under your legs, so that you can sit comfortably with the cuffs in your lap—cops don't like that.

❐ 335. Get a ticket.
☠ ☠ ☠

Any ticket. Jaywalking, speeding, parking, whatever. I got a smoking ticket, once. No kidding. I was smoking in a prohibited zone. Most expensive cigarette I've ever smoked.

❐ 336. Fight the ticket in court.
☠ ☠ ☠ ☠

Courts are spooky, weird places. They're meant to be. You're not supposed to be comfortable in court—you're not supposed to be in court. Court is for when you weren't able to do something without legal intervention. So fighting a ticket in court can be pretty creepy, too. But you can—this is America. Just make sure you're right; the legal system really hates it if you try to fight a ticket you deserved.

❐ 337. Bring a pet to a place that is completely inappropriate or prohibited.
☠ ☠ ☠

Like, say, a dog in an institution of higher learning. Or a rat in a restaurant. Or a reptile wherever. Doing something daring is usually pretty risky, but it's you taking the risk, and you can control yourself to a great extent. You'll never know how an animal, however, will react. Much more risky.

☐ 338. The next time some missionaries come to your door, find out which supernatural being they're peddling, ask them to wait a moment while you bring the dog inside, then call out the name of their deity as if it were the name of your pet.

☐ 339. Wear an article of clothing that will offend the sensibilities of the majority of people you will encounter.

There are entire companies dedicated to selling merchandise to accomplish this. Teenagers do it constantly. Of course, teens are also stupid enough to say stuff like, "Hey, dude, don't judge me by what I wear," when they specifically selected a given piece of apparel for the express purpose of looking different from everybody else. Don a shirt entitled "Official Breast Inspector" before attending a women's rights conference. Put on a Viet Cong lapel pin when you head on over to the local VFW. You get the idea.

☐ 340. Streak.

There is something to be said for moving about without clothing; it's liberating, of course, in the sense that you become truly free of restraint. Restraint of clothing, that is. You also become a lot more susceptible to the elements. Hey, it's your liberation—do with it what you will. Reports of streaking go as far back as 1970 at Princeton University, and 1972 at Notre Dame. Many colleges have seen this fad come and go. And come. And go.

☐ 341. Tell a lie.
☠ – ☠ ☠ ☠ ☠ ☠, depending on conditions

You don't want to make a habit of this; it's much harder to keep track of lies than the truth, and it's quite possible they will convene in an awkward manner and trip you up. So select specific instances where a big, beautiful lie will do the trick, and reserve the practice for those occasions.

☐ 342. Lie to someone you care about deeply.
☠ ☠ ☠ – ☠ ☠ ☠ ☠ ☠,
depending on conditions

This is ugly and insidious. Odds are, you won't get away with it, and the misery, even if you pull it off, will often outweigh the brutality of the punishment you would have faced, had you just told the truth from the get-go. Unless, of course, you're a sociopath.

☐ 343. Lie to a law enforcement official.
☠ ☠ ☠ ☠

Really, really stupid. Odds are, this will come back to bite you on the ass. Even if you forget about it, it ain't likely they will.

☐ 344. Lie to a complete stranger.
☠

This can be a lot of harmless fun, if you're doing it without malice or intent to gain something. I'm sure you've encountered

strangers who jump from exchanging banal pleasantries to offering you incredibly detailed accounts of their personal life. Worse, they ask you impolitely detailed personal questions, even though you've just met them. In that case, you are perfectly excused for creating an entirely fictional character, a nonperson whose personal foibles and predilections you are utterly willing to share with anyone. To best approach this, start out fairly reasonable, then gradually build up your persona's exploits to a ludicrous degree, until the feats are so outlandish that only the most chowder-headed twit could possibly believe.

☐ 345. Visit a juvenile detention center.
☠ ☠

See all those nice kids? Aren't they clean and neat and respectful? Yeah, well many of them are hardened little thugs who have committed some of the most brutal and vile acts you can imagine. It's shocking—each of these kids look too good for that. They look like they're just kids. They probably could be . . . if we could get them away from their parents.

☐ 346. Visit a prison.
☠ ☠ ☠

This is the real deal. A prison seems surreal, because it is probably the only place on the planet specifically designed to diminish every natural urge, need, and craving of the human spirit. It looks like it, too. If you feel totally despondent and ill-at-ease while walking around, that was the intent.

□ 347. Spend time in a juvenile detention center or prison, as an inmate or guard.

☠ ☠ ☠ ☠

You really, really don't want to spend any more time here than is absolutely necessary. It's not fun—it's supposed to be the opposite of fun. Get out as soon as you can.

□ 348. Escape from a prison.

☠ ☠ ☠ ☠ ☠

This can involve a complex plan involving twine, the patrol schedule, a tunnel, and a small aerial vehicle made from styrofoam cups and rubber bands, or it can be a straightforward matter of running off from a work detail. Your choice. There are plenty of types of prisons, too. . . . High school might reasonably be considered a prison, as can many relationships.

□ 349. Interview a killer.

☠ ☠ ☠

All sorts of people have actually killed another person: soldiers, cops, security personnel, homeowners who act in self-defense, etc. But for real daring, you have to sit down and have a conversation with a murderer. This is not easy, as murderers are necessarily creepy. That's part of the reason they're murderers.

□ 350. Attend a rave.

☠ ☠

You know, those crazy, quasi-legal gatherings involving heavy use of Ecstasy and lots of ultraviolet lighting. A rave, dude. For, like, techno music and glow lights. And to appease that adolescent angst you never really kicked. Supposedly, there's a way to find these oft-illicit gatherings by following codes found in your local newspaper, but damned if I can figure it out.

❒ 351. Crash a party.

☠

Sometimes you can accomplish this completely by accident. You've wandered into a club/restaurant/meeting place, and there are people gathered there, drinking, laughing, having a generally good time. You can blend right in. Just don't bring down the fun—that's the only rule for attending a party when you weren't invited.

❒ 352. Join the military.

☠ ☠ ☠

Doesn't have to be active duty; it can be reserve or guard. But active duty is really jumping in with both feet. For details, contact your local recruiter.

❒ 353. Do a ride-along with the police department.

☠

Contact your local law enforcement department for scheduling. This is prurient voyeurism at its utmost; nothing else quite lets you rub your shoulders gently up against the grit—without getting any on yourself, of course. You have no reason for being there. You should probably be more honest with yourself and go watch some porn instead.

354. Join a volunteer fire department.

☠ – ☠ ☠ ☠ ☠, depending on duties performed

There is probably nothing nobler than running into a burning building to save people trapped inside. If you can't swing that, the fire department probably still needs people to do paperwork, sweep up the place, and answer the phone. The nobility is only somewhat diminished for these support duties.

355. Buy a homeless person lunch.

☠ ☠

Stay and watch what happens.

356. Cook a meal for twelve or more people.

☠ ☠

Even if you can cook, you're really looking at something daunting here. . . . It's not just a matter of scaling up your normal recipes; the kind of volume required doesn't allow for that kind of easy modification. No, this is going to push you to your limits, taking up all your counter space, every pot and pan, and the entirety of your fridge.

357. Try to save someone's life.

☠ ☠ – ☠ ☠ ☠ ☠ ☠,

depending on circumstances

For something involving pure coincidence, there are a surprising number of opportunities available; people are constantly having heart seizures, choking, falling, or drowning. You might want to learn CPR, lifeguard swimming, some first aid, and the Heimlich. Suggestion: After intervening in a possibly deadly situation, get away as soon as possible. It's quite possible to hurt someone while saving them, and people have a really weird sense of gratitude . . . which often involves litigation.

☐ 358. Intervene to prevent a crime.

☠ ☠ ☠ ☠

If more citizens just acted to uphold the law, there would probably be a lot less crime. Of course, there would probably be many more dead would-be heroes, too.

☐ 359. Make a citizen's arrest.

☠ ☠ ☠ ☠ ☠

Every state in the Union has provisions for everyday people to nab lawbreakers. Try to bear this in mind, however: Professional law enforcement officials are not subject, as individuals, to many civil and criminal liabilities that you, as a common citizen, may be subject to, even if you're absolutely correct in making an arrest. Nobody, but nobody, will encourage you to engage in this behavior—including me.

☐ 360. Perpetrate a practical joke.

☠ – ☠ ☠ ☠ ☠ ☠, depending on circumstances

The possibilities abound. You can do something as mundane as a prank phone call, all the way up to creating and executing a hoax of international proportions. Try to bear in mind that being the joker is a lot more fun than being the joke-ee, and that your victims might not find the situation as amusing as you do. Famous practical jokes include H. L. Mencken's fictional account of the history of the bathtub (which still often requires debunking), and the very existence of the character Ali G played by English comic Sacha Baron Cohen.

361. Maintain a straight face while perpetrating a practical joke, even when confronted by the victim.

Not easy. The temptation to give it away, or bust out laughing, is quite daunting.

362. Participate in a scavenger hunt.

— , depending on circumstances
Collect things. Race around. Get goofy with friends. Depending on complexity and duration, scavenger hunts can be fairly easy or damned difficult. They're almost always fun.

363. Attend a rock concert.

The noise. The crowd. Oh—and the music. Jam yourself into a space with a lot of other people, all there to enjoy the sounds of the performer(s) whose tunes you dig. It's a communal thing, and definitely hits you on a primal level.

364. Sit in the front row at a rock concert.

Performers, when performing, do a lot of crazy things. You might catch a piece of concert memorabilia thrown by a performer, or get chosen to join the act onstage, or just get hit with a rock star's sweat. Cool.

☐ 365. Jump into a mosh pit.
☠ ☠ ☠

This is a concert-going practice invented by numbskulled teens. Instead of just listening to the music, or dancing, or holding up a cigarette lighter, these imbeciles enjoy the performance by slamming their bodies into each other. Maybe because they're too clumsy to dance.

☐ 366. Attend a punk concert.
☠ ☠ ☠

A punk concert is like a giant mosh pit. This is difficult to do, because there really aren't any punk bands left anymore. You could probably attend a punk cover band concert, which might be a bit like the same thing. For modern quasi-punk, you might want to catch a Leftover Crack show. I won't be there.

☐ 367. Get front row at a punk concert.
☠ ☠ ☠ ☠

Uhhh . . . there isn't really a "front row," per se, at a punk concert. Because there isn't really any assigned seating. Or seating, for that matter. But if you can wrangle your way up to the area just in front of the stage, you might receive similar benefits as you would at a rock concert, with the creative addition of puke, piss, blood, and aggravated battery.

☐ 368. Refuse to retaliate after you're attacked.
☠ ☠ ☠ ☠ ☠

This takes a determination that is quite superhuman—us

humans usually just hit back. Only extraordinary folks—like, say, Gandhi, or Nelson Mandella—rate on this one.

❒ 369. When attacked, fight back, and demolish your opponent.

☠ ☠ ☠

The human way of settling conflict. This is what the whole of human history suggests is the normal response.

❒ 370. Lick a flagpole in winter.

☠ ☠ ☠

I triple-dog dare you. This is an absolute must, an homage to both the playground and Jean Shepherd, creator of the classic film, *A Christmas Story*, which features a flagpole-licking scene. Too good.

❒ 371. Attend a family reunion.

☠

Not that you really like any of those people. . . . But for a freak of genetics and gestation, you wouldn't even know some of them. But they are your family, and always good for a laugh or two, so give it a whirl. You can always leave early.

❒ 372. Attend a high school reunion.

☠ ☠

Let's be perfectly frank: Regardless of the comments and arguments made by those who purport to speak with authority, life is just like high school. High school is basically a microcosm of the entirety of human existence, sad as that may be. So don't you really want to see how everyone turned out? Don't you want them to see how you turned out?

373. Attend a high school reunion and stay sober.
☠ ☠ ☠

Facing this kind of trauma without the benefit of some anesthesia or other is the zenith of folly.

374. Dispose of a body yourself.
☠ ☠

No—I am not talking about a murder victim, goofus. I'm talking about a loved one, someone who entrusted you to handle the arrangements. So it's legal, okay? Furthermore, although it's not widely publicized, it's completely legal for you to bury your own deceased (or burn them, or float them, or whatever) throughout this great land, as long as you follow your local guidelines for health considerations. So why waste that money on a mortuary and gravesite? Plant Pa out in the back forty, and everyone will be happier (except the mortician and graveyard owner, of course).

375. Act as the witness to an accident.
☠ ☠

Somebody got wrapped up, and you watched it happen. It is now your civic duty to stand around and wait for the authorities to take statements. This really benefits those involved (well, those who weren't negligently responsible, of course), and helps them get their insurance claims in a timely and proper manner. Hey—wouldn't you want someone to help out if you were in an accident . . . if it wasn't your fault? Be prepared to exercise your patience.

❏ 376. Provide first aid to an accident victim.
☠ ☠ ☠

Someone's hurt, and you can do something about it. So you should. Even if you're not a doctor, nurse, or paramedic, and even if you've never had first-aid training, you can still be of service, just by holding the victim's hand and calming them down (assuming his or her hands aren't mangled or something). Carry a handkerchief with you always, and you can provide a nice bandage. Let them keep the hankie. Carry a cell phone, too.

❏ 377. Play a video game.
☠

The apex of our development as a tool-using species, this is the finest form of recreation ever devised. Well, the finest you can participate in solo, without partially disrobing.

❏ 378. Challenge an opponent to a competitive two-player video game.
☠ ☠

Going head-to-head, you have to win by sheer skill—usually with some bravado and tenacity thrown in. This can ruin relationships.

379. Challenge several opponents to a competitive multiplayer video game.

☠ ☠ ☠

This is not so much about playing the game as it is an indulgence in smack-talk (that abusive, invective-filled repartee bandied about during the play of a game, often of the electronic variety; may be typed or verbalized). Smack-talk may be aimed at either the game, your opponents, or various and sundry other targets, such as politicians, objects in the room, innocent children passing by, or combinations thereof.

380. Enlist the aid of a compatriot (or compatriots) in a cooperative video game.

☠ ☠

Playing a game can be hard enough, but when you need two or more players to complete a given task in a game, it can suddenly take on a Sisyphean degree of difficulty—and give you cause to hate your friends.

381. Challenge a fourteen-year-old to a video game competition.

☠ ☠

They've got the hand-eye coordination, the experience, the know-how, and the will to sit still for sixteen hours straight, playing the same game over and over (mostly because they're not getting laid, and need to channel that energy). You think you can take one in a fair fight? Doubtful, friend—doubtful.

382. Testify in court.

☠ ☠ ☠

Yeah, they really want to hear from you, and they really want to hear the truth. You can best serve the commonweal by acting as a witness to a crime: Even though you could probably have more fun spending your time in other ways, and you're opening yourself up to all sorts of risk, this is really the right thing to do, if asked. Give it your best shot.

383. Testify in court against someone dangerous and vindictive.

☠ ☠ ☠ ☠ – ☠ ☠ ☠ ☠ ☠,

depending on circumstances

If you face personal danger in exchange for your testimony, with only the hope of the court's discretion in locking away the object of your declarations, then you are indeed living up to your responsibilities as a citizen.

384. Be deposed.

☠ ☠

Not as grueling as actually standing up in a courtroom and offering your take on a given topic, but still a pretty trying event. Try to come across as somewhat sensible, at least.

385. Attend a meeting of a local government body.

☠ ☠

Although it is eminently tempting, do not bring a pillow. Sure, few things are more boring than sitting through a discussion among your city council regarding what kind of wildflowers to plant along the newly paved road, but snoring is frowned on. Besides, it's sometimes good to know what your elected officials are up to. Keep 'em as honest as you can.

❐ 386. Be the lone voice of reason at a public meeting of a local government body.
☠ ☠ ☠

Somebody has to stand up for what is right, even if nobody else agrees. Is that you?

❐ 387. Be the lone voice of nonsense at a public meeting of a local government body.
☠ ☠ ☠ ☠

Sometimes, politicos and their groupies take themselves far too seriously; someone must try to alleviate that problem. Is that you?

❐ 388. Become a foster parent.
☠ ☠ ☠ ☠

Wow—you've got your work cut out for you. And, no matter how good a job you do, you'll have to deal with the state, just because you were obnoxious enough to volunteer to do something good and right and decent.

❐ 389. Adopt a child.
☠ ☠ ☠ ☠ ☠

Be careful. I'll see you in nineteen years—tell me how it turned out.

❏ 390. Reproduce.

☠ ☠ ☠ ☠ ☠

Okay, it doesn't seem like a big accomplishment, since pretty much everyone in history has done it (which is what gives us history, of course), but when you take into account everything that could go wrong, the cost involved, the duration of the obligation, the lost sleep, and other tradeoffs, this is a grueling, ugly, expensive, hazard-prone activity. If done properly.

❏ 391. Reproduce more than once.

☠ ☠ ☠ ☠ ☠

Repeat for effect.

❏ 392. Be present during human reproduction.

☠ ☠ ☠

I'm referring to the really gross part, the part involving the placenta and such. Not the other gross part, conception.

❏ 393. Create an unconventional means of responding to a distasteful cultural custom.

☠ – ☠ ☠ ☠ ☠, depending on circumstances

There are all sorts of these that have crept into our society over the years. Take, for instance, the inane superstition of offering a benedictory appeal after someone sneezes. Just dumb, archaic behavior. Put a spin on it, and make it your own. Like, instead say, "Good autoimmune-response and bacteriological hunting to you," when someone sneezes.

394. Throw off whatever yoke your parents saddled you with.

☠☠☠☠

Maybe it was a religion, maybe it was a cultural notion, could be a language, or even a ridiculous behavior pattern left over from the country of their ancestors. This can be one of the most difficult to overcome; we're all little sponge-brains when we're young, absorbing whatever idiocy is presented to us. It can take a long period of personal observation and experience before we are able to refute those early nonsensical ravings.

395. Plot, then exact, your revenge.

☠ – ☠☠☠☠☠, depending on circumstances

Somebody's done something to you—oh yes, they have. Something that merits an act of vengeance. So be methodical, and choose a means that is appropriate and of like degree. And, hey—contrary to popular opinion, it is not a dish best served cold; by the time it's cold, revenge is all congealed and unsatisfying. Go for the hot stuff, baby.

396. Observe/participate in an autopsy.

☠☠

There's something that's just, well, creepy about cutting into a human corpse. Most of us try to avoid spending time around dead bodies, as it's just something that is cause for squeamishness. Take a gander at the procedure some time, and see if it's as gross as you've imagined.

397. Start a rumor.

☠ – ☠ ☠, depending on conditions

Anyone can retransmit some misinformation; that's no accomplishment. Starting your very own juicy bit of social infection, well, that's a different story. Try to come up with the kind of meme that will really spread, something that transcends your social circle and subculture, something that will travel the globe. It's much easier today, what with e-mail and the Internet and such, so for a really impressive Thing, try to foment your attack on the public record using only word-of-mouth. Do something original, though; check *www.snopes.com* to ensure that you're not just replicating someone else's rumor.

398. Introduce yourself to a stranger.

☠ ☠

It is quite likely, according to all the knowledge we've gathered from archeological and anthropological study, that the human creature's default decision regarding any other human not known to them is to assume a hostile, fatal stance, with ambush overtures when possible. This is probably because human beings are the most deadly, evil, vicious animals ever devised by nature, and have a proven record of conducting themselves accordingly. So our hereditary hesitancy against gregariousness, supported by our cultural mores toward insulation, are simply another set of defense mechanisms. Don't listen to them—the more people you know, the better your life will be. Trust me on this.

❏ 399. Introduce yourself to a stranger while traveling.

☠ ☠

Someone's sitting right next to you, crammed into that space you'll share for the duration of the trip. It's someone you've never met before, but you'll be amazed how much you have in common. Try to read the signals, though—if the other person doesn't feel like being sociable, shut up and keep to yourself.

❏ 400. Introduce yourself to the new neighbors.

☠ ☠

Whether or not you like it, these people are going to share your immediate geographic area for the foreseeable future. You could try to button up your existence, pretend they don't exist, and adopt an isolationist neighborhood policy. This will work against you, in the long term. At some point, you are going to have to deal with them, probably under circumstances involving duress. Better to act with initiative—go out and confront them before they can pre-empt you. If nothing else, you can always feel superior for the fact that you took the first step.

❏ 401. Pick a fight with a neighbor.

☠ ☠ ☠ ☠

They're going to be near you for a while. . . . You engage in this behavior knowing it's going to cause an uncomfortable arrangement for the duration.

402. Try to meet one of your heroes.

☠ ☠ ☠

I once spent the better part of a day driving around Aspen, Colorado, and its outlying area, trying to find Hunter Thompson's Owl Farm. When I finally made it, the look of the place was more than a bit daunting: Huge, ugly steel sculptures of (what I had to guess were) owls looked down from the property's front gate; the porch was loaded with cages containing loud, smelly snow peacocks; and bullet holes punctured every solid material above ground level. And Hunter wasn't home.

403. Meet one of your heroes.

☠ ☠

You want them to be perfect, just the way you envisioned them: paragons of sense and objectivity, brimming with wisdom, monumentally talented. Most of the time, they're just people. For some reason, that becomes a real kick in the teeth. Oh, like the rest of us are any better, right?

404. Have lunch with a celebrity.

☠ ☠ ☠

Ed McMahon is a gentleman I'd long overlooked, in terms of Utter Coolness. Quite understated, and massively accomplished, he's a class act, all the way around. Prowl Beverly Hills or Las Vegas for your opportunity. Better yet, just send one a letter, as an invitation. If you want to do it easily, just become a journalist.

❏ 405. Have breakfast with a porn star.

☠ ☠ ☠ ☠

Serenity is a sharp lady, and I'm glad I had the opportunity to meet her, in person, fully clothed, and actually talk to her. A polite invite is always nice, but doing the journalism Thing is probably your best bet.

❏ 406. Have dinner with someone you've admired since you were a kid.

☠ ☠ ☠ ☠

It's trying when you discover that, regardless of the astounding talent that person might possess, he or she is so crazy that you might be forced to cripple or kill the subject of your former admiration during the meal, when that person actually experiences a psychotic break and literally goes for your throat. Not that this is sure to occur in every case, but I've been there. And it was uncomfortable.

❏ 407. Meet one of your fans.

☠ ☠ ☠

It is absolutely impossible to live up to the expectations of those who adulate you, especially if the reason you're being adored is something you've created, instead of something you are. The reverent expect you to be perfect, and kind, and wonderful, when you're really just that same jackass you ever were.

408. Enter a contest judged solely (or mainly) on physical attractiveness.

☠ ☠

There are some people who are into extreme forms of sexual fetishism with a large dose of humiliation as the theme; even the kinkiest, wildest, most perverted yokel in the world has no clue what true degradation feels like, and that experience is not born in torture chambers or prisons or anything like that. The most severe form of humiliation is the beauty contest, where voluntary entrants are judged on the basis of their appearance, by other fallible humans.

409. Hitchhike.

☠ ☠

Free transport, right? Your car broke down, you don't have bus fare, you missed the train. So you stick out a thumb and try to bum a ride. In certain parts of the country, this practice is not only legal, but semiformalized: where carpooling is encouraged by government mandate, little cluster spots for "slugs" are arranged. This is looked upon as some quintessential American pastime; it's not. It's the most un-American thing ever devised. A real American drives a car, rides a horse, or walks. Except for Bruce Banner.

410. Pick up a hitchhiker.

☠ ☠

You can forget everything you might have assumed about hitch-hiking, having done your research by watching porno movies. Likewise, you can ditch all the crazed notions set forth in those made-for-TV movies, too. Odds are, you are going to pick up neither a gorgeous sexual dynamo nor a psychopathic serial killer. What you are most likely to get is some scruffy, underwashed European backpacker or common vagrant. Yuck.

☐ 411. Shave using a straight razor.

☠ ☠

There's no need, with modern technology, to expose yourself to the dangers of this activity. And yet, there's a certain cachet in utilizing archaic devices for everyday purposes—it makes a hell of an affectation. Plus, you get a really close shave.

☐ 412. Shave/wax/remove hair from a part of your body where you don't normally shave/wax/remove hair from your body.

Your skull, perhaps. Eyebrows. Other places. You'll get some looks the first few days, but those won't bother nearly as much as the stubble when the stuff starts to regrow.

☐ 413. Radically change your appearance.

☠

Whatever anyone says otherwise, looks are extremely important; we judge each other by outward appearance, both upon first and subsequent meetings. Once you are known as having a certain "look" to you, everyone who knows you expects you to look that way in perpetuity. If you do something fairly minor, such as removing some of the hair from your face or skull, adopting a new mode of dress, or even just using some type of normal cosmetic in a way atypical for you, those who know you will treat you differently (for a while, anyway). It's an interesting phenomenon, and a cool experience.

☐ 414. Radically change your appearance with surgery.

☠ – ☠ ☠ ☠ ☠ ☠, depending on severity

Don't like the way you look? Well, we have the capability to change that. There is virtually no limit to the kinds of modifications currently available to the human form. Try something different, interesting: Get an elephantine trunk placed on your face, or a peacock's feathers at the base of your spine. I mean, if you're going to do it, do it whole hog. Liposuction is passé.

☐ 415. Attend a convention.

☠

Lots of people getting together for a common interest, to talk to each other and listen to still yet more people talk about the topic at hand. Sounds boring, doesn't it? It sure can be. Try to make sure you go to one held in a fun city, so at least your nonconvention time isn't wasted.

☐ 416. Attend a convention of fanatics.

☠ ☠

Comic books. Guns. Science fiction. Cars. Southern Baptists. People are completely batshit about their particular fetish, and they just love to congregate with other crazed adherents of their respective mania. If you throw yourself into the mix, prepare yourself to either get swept up with their crazed glorification or ripped to shreds by an angry mob. Might I suggest the Small Press Expo (*www.spxpo.com*)? Yes, I am a geek.

❒ 417. Take up a drastically annoying habit, such as picking your nose or playing the accordion.

☠ ☠

Go out in public. Practice your new hobby among strangers. Best employed on public transportation.

❒ 418. Try being homeless for a month or more.

☠ ☠ ☠

Sleep in your car. No car? Go from shelter to shelter, looking for open beds. There's always the traditional cardboard box or steam grate. Beg for food and sustenance however you can. Go Dumpster-diving. Don't bother with personal hygiene—I mean, hey, you're homeless. Nobody expects you to smell like roses. At least you'll save time getting ready in the morning.

❒ 419. Visit a current battlefield/war zone.

☠ ☠ ☠ ☠ ☠

Think this one through first. Because you'd be going to a place where people are actually trying to kill other people. On purpose. This sounds like a really bad idea. Luckily, at any given time, there happen to be twenty-nine or so available on the planet, so you don't need to make reservations.

PART 1 PUBLIC THINGS

❏ 420. Visit a historic battlefield/war zone.
☠

You might have read about the conflict in school, or seen a fictionalized account in a movie or on television. It's unlikely, however, you will be prepared for one amazing aspect of this bygone battle: the proximity in which combatants used to fight. When you think of grand battles and dramatic, horrific warfare, it's easy for your brain to extrapolate these things into a huge scale, a size to match the numbers of the dead and the fury of the fight. Often, you'll be astounded when you really see the place: It's usually pretty small—those folks had to get right up next to each other for the killing. That, in itself, is harrowing.

❏ 421. Visit Gettysburg.
☠

Get this: It was a big, bloody war, the worst in American history, in terms of American deaths, with over 600,000 Americans dead. Gettysburg was arguably the most devastating battle, as casualties were being tallied at the rate of one per second on the second day of the engagement.

❏ 422. Go to the top of Masada.
☠ ☠ ☠ ☠

Combine a fascination with history, the danger of heights, and the inanity of walking around in the desert, all in one fell swoop. Learn the story of how a bunch of crazed, right-wing persons of Hebraic intent engaged in the one of the most un-Jewish acts ever—committing suicide after massacring everyone who lived in the fortress. Look down on the remains of the Roman encampments built for the siege, and the ramp they built up the side of the mountain, stone by stone. Ugly, spooky, and powerful.

☐ 423. Visit a hospice/nursing home/veterans' hospital on any holiday.
☠ ☠ ☠ ☠

This is not a dare about feeling good. And it's damn sure not a dare about making others feel good. No, this is about challenging yourself: Go ahead, go and have a look. See what it looks like to be alone, to be warehoused at the tail end of life. This is an optimum moment to decide how you're going to plan for your later days: Accumulate wealth so that you can pay for people to surround you with comfort and praise; breed manically, in the hopes one or more of your spawn will take care of that aspect of your endgame; ensure that you have a game plan, based on either age or condition, for when you will peacefully and responsibly check yourself out of Chez Life; or possibly some other option I haven't considered.

☐ 424. Litter.
☠

Just chuck whatever is in your hand into the street/lane/sidewalk/ground. That's where it belongs. That's where it will go, even if you follow the advice of those who insist on "proper disposal." *Proper disposal* is another phrase for "landfill," which is a rather fancy-pants way of saying "we're chucking it into the ground." Which is littering. Duh.

☐ 425. **Spend eight hours straight holding a cardboard sign at a busy intersection.**

☠ ☠

It can read anything you want: "Honk if you like my butt," "Will work for Spam," or "Jesus Saves"—you get the idea. You will be amazed at a particular phenomenon, which eludes all psychological examination. Some people—total strangers!—will stop and give you money.

☐ 426. **While free from any infestation of your own offspring, baby-sit someone else's.**

☠ ☠ ☠

You will never find a more demanding, stressful, infuriating activity. Try it for a minimum of six hours to get the full effect. This is quite possibly the best form of birth control ever devised—try it on your partner whenever he or she gets the bug to get some wee-beasties of your own.

☐ 427. **Go to one of those "Anonymous" meetings (pick your favorite: Alcoholics, Narcotics, Funaholics, etc.), and just antagonize the heck out of everyone there.**

☠ ☠ ☠

When your turn comes around, introduce yourself, and say, "I've been _____-free for one day." Then, when they all clap for you, say something like, "Yeah, last night I had sooooo much _____, it was really amazing. I mean, I was just having _____ all over the place. Really. All kinds of it. And I was kinda thinking about doing it again tonight. I mean, I can always quit tomorrow, anyway. So tonight seems like a great time to just really go all-out and indulge in good, sweet, yummy _____."

❏ 428. Create a panic.
☠ ☠ ☠

There are different ways to induce mass hysteria. You could set off the fire alarm in a building. Spread a rumor about the imminent outbreak of a virulent disease. Or the classic calling-"fire"-in-a-crowded-theater. This is completely illegal, and may now even land you on some terrorist watch list.

❏ 429. Create a pilot for your own reality-TV show.
☠ ☠ ☠

So, you think your life is interesting? Is it interesting enough that other people would want to watch it? Is it interesting enough that somebody will pay you to let other people watch it? Maybe . . . . Good luck. Every now and then, various media outlets offer a chance to do this.

❏ 430. Give someone personal advice.
☠ ☠ ☠

Okay, so maybe you think you know a little something about life. Maybe you've been down a road or two, or several other aphorisms. And you've got this friend/acquaintance/ex-lover who wants your take on a particular situation. Actually—that person doesn't really want your input: he says he does, but what he really wants is to talk about his problem, and how he is going to avoid or exacerbate it—that person will never follow your advice and solve the damned thing. Deal with that.

431. Try to tell someone, politely, that his or her significant other is not a good match for him or her.

☠ ☠ ☠ ☠

This is incredibly difficult to do if you have respect for either party involved. Try to be accurate and methodical, and come off as sincerely as possible. And no, trying to break someone up just so you can sleep with either party yourself does not count.

432. Engage in a game of mumblety-peg.

☠ ☠ ☠

You throw or drop a knife and try to make it stick, blade-first, into the ground. Your opponents must mimic your technique. Groovy. And a cute way to perforate your foot.

433. Act as a mediator for opposing parties.

☠ ☠

Sure, everyone's just talking. And you don't even have a dog in the fight. For some reason, if you have any judgment skills whatsoever, it will probably become rapidly apparent to you that one side, if not both, is full of poo-poo/ka-ka. Try to stay evenhanded.

434. Rob a grave.

☠

Our culture looks upon this practice as incredibly egregious. I'm not sure why. Burying someone with valuables seems bizarre. If you extrapolate an infinite number of people (first living, then dead), each taking only, for sake of argument, a trivial memento into the ground with them, the rest of us would eventually have nothing left above ground. Moreover, a good percentage of historical, scientific, and artistic "finds" are either actual acts of grave-robbing, or the fruits of a previous grave-robbing expedition. With that justification, go have fun in a cemetery. Although it's illegal, of course.

❒ 435. Serve on a committee.
☠ ☠ ☠ ☠

You'll quickly learn just how slowly a group effort can move, and how long it takes to accomplish anything. Bring a book to read.

❒ 436. Be a total iconoclast, rejecting the social norm, in at least one thing.
☠ ☠ ☠ ☠ ☠

It's sad but true: the most dangerous things, the things most difficult to accomplish, are often not of physical composition and hindrance, but the restrictions and taboos we get from our culture. Often, pushing against these things is far more challenging than a feat of skill, prowess, or cunning: this is true bravery. Being an Other is daunting to most people.

❒ 437. Cultivate a distaste for something everyone else seems to like.
☠ ☠ ☠

Say, children, or puppies. But, c'mon, really—who are you fooling? What kind of sick bastard hates puppies?

❏ 438. Acquire a taste for something everyone else seems to dislike.

🕱 🕱 🕱 🕱

The end cut, or the fat, off a roast. The smell of industrial waste. Dating Scientologists. You get the idea.

❏ 439. Live with a lover.

🕱 🕱 🕱

There's been a taboo about this in our culture for a considerable amount of time. You get to see if your lover is one of those annoying people who squeezes the toothpaste tube the wrong way. Yes, much of the romance might leave the relationship—but you can find out if there's anything else of substance to keep you together.

❏ 440. Never get married, even though you have a significant other.

🕱 🕱 🕱 🕱

Our society hates this. Everyone really wants you to be married—mainly because they are married and can't stand the notion of anyone else escaping the curse. Of course, in actuality, there's very little reason to do so, but many reasons not to. Financially, marriage is a tax burden, and a method of losing everything in one fell swoop (the two of you are twined, inseparably). Legally, you're both one person, which hinders your combined ability to accomplish certain things; if you stay single, you can both purchase your own property and get much better rates than if you were linked. Plus, no matter what else, you won't have a spouse! If for no other reason, dodge this bullet.

☐ 441. Never get married, even if you end up without a significant other because of it.
☠ ☠ ☠ ☠

At a certain point in your life, it becomes much easier to just settle down with another marriage-minded person who has given up his or her ideals and desires, in exchange for the dubious benefits of capitulating to social norms. This is a cop-out. Anyone who won't stay with you because you don't want to get married would end up being one lousy, terrible spouse. Sometimes, yes, it is better to be alone.

☐ 442. Remain child-free.
☠ ☠ ☠ ☠ ☠

The vast majority of our society is geared toward the creation, maintenance, financial sustenance, and sensibilities of children. This is inane and bass-ackwards: A culture built for children is wasted on those that lack the potential to appreciate it, and disenfranchises those who make it possible. Nearly everyone will get on your case if you refuse to play along. Screw them. Leave the propagation of the species to those who have no other means to fill their empty lives. In response to that bromide about using children as a form of retirement support, feel free to point out that such a thing is not guaranteed in the slightest and that you could easily use the money you'll save by not having kids to afford professional, loyal servants who will perform the necessary tasks in a much better manner.

443. Halt all communication with a family member.

☠ ☠ ☠

Sometimes, the right thing for you, personally, is a practice that society frowns on—distancing yourself from a relative. Screw society: Do what you gotta do.

Live in a nation that . . .
444. . . . has a democracy.

☠ ☠

Basically, a bunch of people getting together to decide who promised them the best stuff, then letting that person make decisions for them. A real nice way to let a bunch of idiots pick things you'd never want and don't need. Plus, you get to suffer through the wrong ideas that happen to be popular with the majority of the time, which will finally get fixed long after you're dead (America has a wonderful track record of such things, such as slavery, prohibition of alcohol, segregation, incarcerating citizens of a certain race or creed, etc.). Still, the best thing available.

445. . . . has a monarchy.

☠ ☠ ☠

Someone slept with someone else, and their kid is now, theoretically, the individual most capable of telling everybody else what to do. Not the most progressive of modern institutions, I'd have to say.

☐ 446. . . . has a theocracy.

☠ ☠ ☠ ☠

Somebody's been listening to voices in their head and has decided they come from a supernatural being of some sort. Instead of locking that person up, we let them dictate rules for existence, commerce, and culture to the rest of us. This is not for grownups. (*Extra Bonus:* Live in a theocratic society, even though you don't belong to the state-sanctioned religion.)

☐ 447. . . . has some form of collectivism.

☠ ☠ ☠ ☠ ☠

Oh, there are plenty of Ideal Societies from which to choose: fascism, communism, socialism. . . . Aren't they neat? Don't they make a lot of sense? Wouldn't it be swell not to worry about things like hunger or money or independent thought? Sure—if you don't mind a diet that consists primarily of oatmeal and a culture that venerates the aesthetic pleasures of four-hour operatic epics about self-sharpening plows.

☐ 448. . . . suffers under a police state.

☠ ☠ ☠ ☠ ☠

Congrats! You now live in the safest place on the planet. Feel free to walk down dark alleys at all hours of the day or night, or even through the parks of major metropolitan centers whenever you feel like it, carelessly brandishing your valuables and leaving your car unlocked. There's no risk of loss, no danger to your own self, because the police run everything, and anyone even suspected of being a criminal is quietly removed from polite society. Great . . . until someone suspects or accuses you.

PART 1 PUBLIC THINGS

❏ 449. . . . is under the rule of a dictator.
☠ ☠ ☠ ☠ ☠

The simplest, most straightforward plan for governing the interaction of human beings; one person (usually the toughest), makes all the rules and reaps all the benefits. Not a bad arrangement—if you're the dictator.

❏ 450. Go without toilet paper for a week.
☠ ☠ ☠

Of all the wonders and comforts afforded us, from making fire to genetic manipulation, it might suck most to not have toilet paper. Toilet paper is magic.

❏ 451. Survive a stabbing.
☠ ☠ ☠ ☠

The human body is a big mushy bag full of liquids. If you puncture that bag, or any of the many bags tucked inside (like so many gooey Russian nesting dolls), bad, bad things will happen, the very least of which is having the slop drip out; the liquids can merge and mix, which is more than awful. Do your best to avoid any punctures.

❏ 452. Survive a gunshot wound.
☠ ☠ ☠ ☠ ☠

Guns are designed to chuck a piece of metal at a target, at speeds high enough to punch a hole in it. We know this. It is also important to understand that a human body does not withstand holes created by high-velocity metal very well; in addition to the damage the piece of metal makes in its own right, there are all sorts of additional concerns, such as hydrostatic shock, sepsis, bone shrapnel, etc. Understanding this is important because you never want to endure it. If you do, and survive, you are quite lucky.

❒ 453. Survive a bite.

☠☠ – ☠☠☠☠☠, depending on conditions
Mouths are chock-full of all sorts of bacteria and other microbial nasties, as well as sharp, jagged teeth. They can pierce, tear, and rend. Bites do not heal well, and they become infected easily and leave horrific scars. Get good treatment, as soon as possible.

❒ 454. Survive a human bite.

☠☠☠ – ☠☠☠☠☠,
depending on conditions
Of biters, humans have the most and worst microbes in their mouths. Nasty.

❒ 455. Survive a snakebite.

☠☠☠ – ☠☠☠☠☠,
depending on conditions
Snake venom is pretty deadly. But poisonous snakes only get one or two good shots in, and those are fanged attacks, which make nice, neat little holes, and antivenin for snakes common to any geographical area is usually available in medical centers nearby. Snakes without fangs, such as constrictors, have rings of sharp cartilage "teeth," designed to penetrate the skin and flesh of their prey, and snag there. There are also plenty of

135

exotic and dangerous bacteria inside a nonvenomous snake's mouth. Finally, many nonvenomous snakes have saliva that contains anticoagulants, creating wounds that bleed profusely for a long time. Getting bitten by a snake is no picnic.

☐ 456. Encounter a demented person.

☠ – ☠ ☠ ☠ ☠ ☠, depending on conditions

Nut-jobs abound—the simple fact of the matter is that there are far more people who have insane ideas, perceptions, and opinions than are currently undergoing treatment or are locked away for committing dangerous acts. It's quite trying for most of us to deal with these people, because we are hindered by the double detriment of personal sanity and a desire to remain somewhat polite, while they are not likewise limited.

☐ 457. Converse with a demented person on the telephone.

☠ ☠

If you get into a conversation with one of these people on the telephone, do your best to keep them away from topics that might exacerbate their descent into their own brand of dementia, and thus keep you on the phone longer. These might include, but are not limited to: space aliens, the government of this or any other country, law enforcement entities, any portion of the electromagnetic spectrum, extrasensory abilities, or any type of sexuality. The nice part about dealing with them on the telephone is that you can always hang up.

❏ 458. Converse with a demented person over the Internet.
☠

Even better than the phone, with Internet communication exchanges, you can simply ignore the person with the mental instability. You are not forced into any semblance of truly human interaction, as you won't even hear the timbre and inflection of their voice.

❏ 459. Deal with someone demented, in person.
☠ ☠ ☠ – ☠ ☠ ☠ ☠ ☠,
depending on conditions

This is a lot trickier, as there is the constant possibility that the person in question will become so completely bonkers that he or she might become aggressive and attack you physically. Watch out for that.

❏ 460. Deal with a demented person to whom you are related.
☠ ☠ ☠ ☠ – ☠ ☠ ☠ ☠ ☠,
depending on conditions

It's quite likely that someone related to you, in some respect or other, is off his or her noggin. Your difficulties are therefore multiplied exponentially, because you have to be extra polite and careful when handling this person.

461. Live among a culture wholly distinct from yours, with a primitive people.

The greatest of anthropological challenges, this is the baseline from which all other societal norms are measured. To think that you could stay among these people and not impact their notions of their own society is ludicrous; trying to do so, in an effort to keep their own culture "intact," is absurd, and just as monstrous as anything they might do out of habit or tradition. Consider France.

462. Attend a Greek festivity.

This will involve some of the best-tasting food on the planet, plenty of alcoholic beverages, some dark, gorgeous people, and—no kidding—a lot of broken flatware. I'm not sure quite how that last part became an element of celebratory activities, but it's enjoyable enough to really make an event special.

FINANCIAL THINGS

They say money can't buy you happiness. They are chumps. While happiness might not be available on the store shelf right next to the deodorant and masking tape, it is one heck of a lot easier to be happier with money than without it. And, as adult behavior in a civilized world demands a constant exercise of informed decision-making, you continually are putting your money—and happiness—at risk. Do proper cost-benefit analysis. Stay rational and objective. Hire a professional. You might still lose everything, anyway.

❏ 463. Apply for a job.

For some reason, we place a great deal of stress upon ourselves during this process, as if the possible rejection is in some serious way a reflection of our own merits as human beings. Which, usually, it isn't.

❏ 464. Apply for a job for which you have no inherent or learned skills, talent, or disposition.

Hey—the worst they can say is "no."

❏ 465. Apply for a job for which you're hopelessly overqualified and overeducated.

It is always interesting to see if a rocket scientist will be hired as a short-order cook. Not surprisingly, most often the astrophysicist doesn't get to flip burgers.

❏ 466. Quit your job.

Walking away from a continual source of sustenance and support is an incredibly difficult thing to do. Even in the best circumstances, there is always a feeling of panic and plenty of room for second-guessing. This is extremely worthwhile.

PART 1 PUBLIC THINGS

❏ 467. Quit your job in dramatic fashion.

☠ ☠ ☠

Tell your boss to do something anatomically impossible. Joyously shout your renouncement of your soon-to-be-former employer in full view and hearing of your colleagues. Burn your bridges, and make sure you torched 'em good. Walk away from this knowing that door is closed forever.

❏ 468. Quit your job without having another lined up.

☠ ☠ ☠ ☠

Sometimes, well, sometimes you really can't stand what you're doing on a day-to-day basis. You loathe waking each morning, because it means another stretch of doing something you find utterly reprehensible. Nothing is worth that—no amount of money can make up for the misery you're going through. Just pull the plug and walk away; you probably won't starve, and you can always find something else.

❏ 469. Quit your job without having another lined up, move to another country without a visa, and start from scratch.

☠ ☠ ☠ ☠ ☠

Nearly every country on the planet has its own rules for allowing foreigners to live there and work. These rules are pretty strict and difficult to avoid. If you didn't know it before, you've read it here, so now you know. Not to say that it can't be done. . . .

470. Get fired from your job.

☠ ☠ ☠ ☠

I go back and forth on this: I got "laid off" one time, along with fourteen other people, when my company's budget was shrinking. . . . Does that mean I got fired? Good question. Here's what I think: If you're going to get fired, do something spectacular to be fired for. It sure would have saved me a lot of questions down the road. . . .

471. Hire someone.

☠ ☠ ☠

You'd be surprised—there aren't a lot of good people out there. Scratch that—there may be plenty of good people out there, but there sure aren't a lot of good employees available. Probably because the good ones are all already employed. You take a risk when you bring someone into your business; you are giving that person a position of trust and responsibility, no matter what that position might be. In turn, you are responsible for that individual, which is no mean duty. He or she is now your envoy, whether you like it or not.

472. Fire someone.

☠ ☠ ☠ ☠

You'd be amazed how many sundry difficulties this brings into play, even when the action is totally appropriate. It can often cause almost as many problems as it solves. A crying shame.

❏ 473. Gamble.

☠

You throw the dice or play the cards or pull the handle. Repeat
for effect.

❏ 474. Gamble in Vegas.

☠ ☠ ☠

This is the big-time. The no-kidding, how-you-do-it, down-and-
dirty way to wager. You've got a system? Great—see all those
big buildings with all the flashing lights and fancy gewgaws?
Those were built by money taken from people with "systems."
But go ahead and try, anyway. Hey, it's only money, right?

❏ 475. Gamble in Atlantic City.

☠ ☠

To add to the thrill, don't park your vehicle in a casino lot, but
instead in a public space. Walk to it after dark.

❏ 476. Gamble in South America.

☠ ☠ ☠

I was at a small, intimate casino, where the croupiers all wore
tuxedoes and spoke about as much English as I did Spanish.
There were even a couple of games I didn't know how to play,
but everyone was quite helpful, and very patient, and treated
me like a valued customer. Out front, there was a guy at the door
dressed in full battle armor, carrying a submachine gun.

❑ 477. Gamble in Holland.

☠

For a country that has taken the pleasures of sex, drugs, and rock 'n' roll to a high art, they pretty much suck at hosting gambling. Which is really okay; if you've got sex, drugs, and rock 'n' roll, what need is there for gambling?

❑ 478. Gamble in an inane manner at a tableful of very serious gamblers.

☠ ☠ ☠ ☠

Make some crazy bets, giggle a lot, and talk to everyone, whether or not they respond.

❑ 479. Gamble in an illegal setting.

This is one of those "victimless" crimes . . . assuming you don't do the wrong thing, or end up in the wrong place at the wrong time—then you could, quite feasibly, become the victim. Of course, just by going to an illegal gambling venue, you're pretty much assuring that you're in the wrong place.

☠ ☠ ☠ ☠ ☠

❑ 480. Play at least one game against a pool shark.

☠ ☠

We're talking billiards here: eight-ball, nine-ball, etc. Not an actual shark in a swimming pool, of course. Play to lose, and see what your opponent does. . . . Pool sharks are conditioned to let the "mark" (you) win the first couple of games, so as to get you to bet more money. This can be fun.

☐ 481. Start your own business.

✖ ✖ ✖ ✖

America is the land of opportunity. It was started with the notion that everyone should be allowed to make as much money as possible, and the best way to do that is to start your own business. But—starting your own business can also be a pretty sure-fire way to lose all your money. According to the Small Business Administration, one out of every three new businesses fail in the first four years of existence.

☐ 482. Go into business with a friend.

✖ ✖ ✖ ✖

How long will that person remain your friend, once personal finances are involved? If you can pull this off, you're a couple of exceptional people, no doubt about it.

☐ 483. Go into business with a family member. There are those who say stuff like, "Blood is thicker than water."

✖ ✖ ✖ ✖

Okay, but is it thicker than your bankbook? This is a good way to get out of having to deal with your family ever again.

☐ 484. Tell the IRS that they're wrong.

✖ ✖ ✖ ✖

They just love to hear that. They have entire departments full of people dedicated to helping you resolve your problem. Sadly, all those departments and all those people are given the assistance of lots and lots of computers, all specifically designed to follow processes that will make it nearly impossible for them to change any incorrect information in your file, while faithfully preserving all incorrect information about you until the end of time.

☐ 485. Buy a house.
☠ ☠ ☠

This is an awkward, complicated, nerve-wracking process impeded by the best efforts of an entire industry created to take whatever money it can from you, in all sorts of undeserved ways. The real estate agents, the lawyers, the appraisers, the mortgage brokers, the quasi-government "loan-guarantee" institutions—they all want to take a little taste of your American pie. And we let them, only because the vast amounts of paperwork we have to deal with when purchasing a house totally boggles our minds, giving them the time to swoop in and carve out a piece, like vultures.

☐ 486. Buy a house in a foreign country.
☠ ☠ ☠ ☠

This can be an interesting experiment: Take out a stopwatch at the beginning of the process and try to find out exactly how long it takes you to get screwed.

☐ 487. Sell a house.
☠ ☠ ☠ ☠

This is almost always a bad idea. If you can, avoid it. You'll never get as much as you thought you were going to, even if it sells at a higher price than you asked, after all the taxes and fees and commissions and whatnot. Much better to keep it and rent it out.

488. Rent out a house.

☠ ☠ ☠

Oh, you wanted an exercise in pain? Here you go. Try renting to what starts as a small family, which incrementally grows into a large, extended "family" over a short period of time—a family comprised of the sort of people who threaten the neighbors with machetes, and who claim that they've already paid their rent, even when they clearly haven't.

489. Rent an apartment.

☠ ☠ ☠

Sure, you're giving a bunch of money to the owner of the property, with no long-term reward for yourself. But you are not beholden to anyone, either, and you're not tied down to a specific location or investment. You're footloose and free and all that jazz.

490. Buy a car.

☠ ☠ ☠

For some reason, this has become a grueling process for every-one involved—including the customer. This is an utterly ridicu-lous situation: You want to buy something, the vendor wants to sell it to you, but there's an annoying little dance we must perform before completing the transaction, and even more she-nanigans involving your state and local governments afterward.

491. Buy a used car.

☠ ☠

Common understanding suggests that purchasing a used vehicle is a means of acquiring someone else's problems. Yet, on the flip side, common understanding also declares that a new vehicle loses up to one-third of its value when driven off the dealer's lot. Both, sadly, are true.

☐ 492. Lease a car.
☠ ☠ ☠ ☠

If you'd like to start a lifelong practice of never owning anything yourself, outright, here's a great place to start.

☐ 493. Sell a car.
☠ ☠ ☠

You never really know what people are like until you try to sell them something. Random and diverse strangers will contact you, soon after you've announced to the world that you're selling the car. Every now and then you stumble across the decent sort. Well, at least I did—you might not be so lucky. Have fun at the DMV.

☐ 494. Work in a freelance capacity, for more than a month.
☠ ☠ ☠

Without a steady paycheck, it's hard to plan ahead. And in the world of freelance, even with "guaranteed" contracts worked out in advance, you are still at the discretion of the customer, who may or may not pay you in due time. The longer you do this, the easier it becomes, as you will have a nice backlog of receivables waiting for you.

PART 1 PUBLIC THINGS

147

☐ 495. Attend a live auction.

☠ ☠

The operative word of this Thing is live—not virtual, not online, but LIVE. You actually have to pick your butt up and go somewhere to do this. Once there, bid on something. Do not drink—buzzed bidding is directly responsible for over half the inane auction purchases in this country alone. The big dare of this activity is to leave without having purchased anything.

☐ 496. Bid at a live auction.

☠

Not as difficult as simply attending and not bidding.

☐ 497. Bid at a live auction, and give up when usurped by a counter-bid.

☠ ☠

Just about as tough as not bidding at all. . . . Giving up something you want, when someone else is bidding against you, goes against the grain of our internal hunter-gatherer instinct. Auctioneers know this, which is why auctions exist.

☐ 498. File a lawsuit.

☠ ☠

It's the modern American hobby. There are an unlimited amount of reasons you can sue someone. Try to keep in mind that the only people who win lawsuits are the lawyers.

☐ 499. Turn down a reasonable settlement offer.

☠ ☠ ☠

You might regret this later.

☐ 500. File a claim.

☠ ☠

There is nothing special you have to do: just announce to who-ever it is that you think owes you something that you want to collect, and see if that person or company will give it to you. They might not, but hey, sometimes they will. Be reasonable and courteous.

☐ 501. Negotiate a contract.

☠ ☠

Contrary to popular belief, everything is negotiable. The terms of your mortgage, your car financing, even an oath of office are all contracts you are free to enter (or not enter); you can change the terms of those contracts as you see fit. Hey, the worst the other party can do is say "no." You'd be surprised how much folks are willing to concede, if you just ask for it.

☐ 502. While negotiating a contract, make a ludicrously insane request.

☠ ☠ ☠

How will you know exactly how desperate the other party is, unless you test said party with a contractual condition that is totally outside the bounds of reason?

503. Try growing something.

☠

Could be some rare orchids, with which you'll compete in some big orchid-growing contest. Or maybe some tomatoes on stakes behind the place you live. Or maybe a plant in your bedroom closet, with heat lamps and UV light. . . . Whatever it is, you've got to water it and care for it and generally be nurturing. And it still might die.

504. Try growing something for profit.

☠ ☠ ☠ ☠

Okay, Farmer Brown, take your best whack at it. You'll be glad to know that the entire resources of the Department of Agriculture are at your disposal, and you can get crop insurance, and that there are price supports and subsidies for just about everything grown in this country. Not many other business ventures give you a "do-over" if you screw up. Of course, it's also one of the most difficult, grueling, archaic, demeaning ways to raise revenue. More power to you.

505. Barter.

☠

There are those snobs who suggest that bartering is an archaic, unsophisticated form of transaction, and that modern commerce is much more complex. They have it exactly backwards: The reason money is used today is that it makes transactions much simpler and, therefore, much less sophisticated. When all you have is a set of goods, and you want to exchange some of your goods for some of somebody else's, you are dealing with the true high art of the free market. You can also lose your shirt.

❏ 506. Haggle with a vendor at an open-air market.
☠

This should be performed in a foreign country for best effect, where both you and the other party have only cursory knowledge of each other's language, but you can often find similar circumstances in your own state or city. These people are the world's most ideal capitalist entrepreneurs. Check for a price—there probably isn't one. Let them throw out an offer. Ask if that's the best offer. Make a counteroffer. Repeat for effect. Never, ever fall in love with the object you wish to purchase—if you do, you have killed your ability for true negotiation.

❏ 507. Haggle at a Middle Eastern market.
☠ ☠

The people in this region have a multi-thousand-dollar-per-year tradition of quibbling over prices. You think you can get the best of them? Give it your best shot. Good tactics: a willingness to walk away, scoffing, and gesticulating wildly.

❏ 508. Haggle at a Korean market.
☠ ☠

Strangely, it would seem as if a good number of Middle Eastern persons was transported magically to the Korean Peninsula; the tactics, mannerisms, and abilities are frighteningly similar.

❒ 509. Haggle at a South American market.
☠ ☠

There are a lot of smiles exchanged in these transactions—unlike in some other geographic regions, these people actually seem to enjoy the interaction and the thrill of the deal. They'll still gut you if they can, though. Which is only fair.

❒ 510. Haggle at an American flea market.
☠ ☠

They might look like rejects from a casting call for actors with distinguishing hillbilly traits, but these are probably some of the sharpest businesspeople in the country. Not an inch, not a bit will they budge. Good for them.

❒ 511. Conduct cold-call sales over the phone.
☠

Go ahead—bother people at home, or at their place of work. Ask them if they want something they obviously don't need. Pester them until they either hang up or buy whatever it is you're selling. At least they can't punch you over the phone.

❒ 512. Conduct cold-call sales door-to-door.
☠

If you're over the age of twelve, this is no longer adorable. In fact, it's just annoying. You are basically trespassing, and for sure pissing people off.

513. Homestead a vacant plot of land.

☠ ☠ ☠ ☠

There are still places on this planet that you can own by simply going there and setting up house. Of course, they're out in the, well, I can't say they're in the middle of nowhere, because that implies that there's some border and shape to "nowhere," which is not the case—these pieces of land are nowhere. You have to go there to own one. Bring soup.

514. Homestead in Alaska.

☠ ☠ ☠ ☠ ☠

Not only do you have to choose a nowhere location, but you also have to pick a cold one. Unfortunately, you have to be a resident of the state to apply for this.

515. Stake a mining claim.

☠ ☠

Yes, it's bizarre, but staking your own claim is not some archaic form of acquiring mining rights, a relic from black-and-white movies about the Gold Rush: You, too, can be a miner, with your own plot of land, just by finding some empty parcel and staking it out ("staking" it means to literally put down stakes at the corners of your plot, designating its location and perimeter). Check your local laws, buy a pickax, and go get rich!

516. Squat on a piece of property.

☠ ☠ ☠

Possibly the lowest form of legalized theft, you can rip off some real estate by just sitting on it for a given length of time. Better hope the rightful owners don't catch you before the time limit expires. Check all local laws.

❏ 517. Trespass.

☠ – ☠ ☠ ☠ ☠ ☠, depending on locale

If you're going to do this, make it grandiose—don't just cut through the neighbor's backyard. Make it a real daring event. Climb the fence of a junkyard protected by attack dogs; wander into a construction site. This is, yes, illegal.

❏ 518. Invest in a stock market.

☠ ☠ ☠ ☠

Don't let anyone tell you differently: Buying and selling openly traded stocks is just like any other form of gambling—there is no guarantee you're going to make money, no matter how you do it. And the term *openly traded* can be a bit of a misnomer, too; often, you need to purchase the services of a broker or agent or arbiter of some sort, which cuts into your profits. There are plenty of stock markets to choose from, from the well-known New York Stock Exchange, to the Tokyo, but you might try the Chicago Stock Exchange, which is a lot less pretentious.

❏ 519. Invest in fine wine.

☠ ☠ ☠ ☠

This is the kind of gamble in which you can take a bath; a metaphorical bath, to be sure, because actually, literally bathing in wine is just silly. If you're really going to do it, you've got to invest in one of those wine cellar things, either a real one in your house or a portable, plug-in type.

520. Take a class in wine appreciation.

This was an elective at my college. The institution offered no credit, but still . . . drinking and learning? Here's the rule from that class: Any wine you like to drink is a Good Wine.

521. Invest in precious metals.

People have been hoarding different kinds of shiny metal ever since some yokel decided it had more inherent value than the other, duller stuff. That is not to say that there aren't some basic chemical and physical properties of, say, gold that aren't pretty nifty. But that doesn't mean that it will continue to command a specific value indefinitely.

522. Invest in commodities.

Sounds fancy, don't it? Well, the word *commodities* is just a highfalutin way of saying "stuff." So, you're buying "stuff." Or, even worse, you're buying the opportunity to sell stuff at a certain price. You better hope your stuff remains valuable—at least as valuable as the price you paid. Otherwise, guess what?

523. Invest in foreign currency.

Okay, get this: you're betting that the price of your money is going to be better (lower or higher, depending on your trade) than some other country's money. Now, how silly is that? Why not just try honest gambling?

❐ 524. Buy someone a gift.

☠ ☠

You think you know someone? Try to find someone a gift—a real gift, not cash, or a gift certificate. See if that person really likes it; your true friends will let you know if you picked right, or if they find the gift nonsensical and useless.

❐ 525. Buy someone a living thing as a gift.

☠ ☠ ☠ ☠

This is one of the riskiest things you can do for someone you love, or even like. They may like it, or they may take offense; this is right up there with demeaning their skills as a lover or yanking bits of their body away from the rest of it without benefit of anesthesia. A pet is a commitment of both time and money, and a heady responsibility—it's a living creature, which will only remain living at the expense (of both time and funds) of the owner. Imposing this on an unsuspecting person can yield unpredictable results.

❐ 526. Invest in fine art.

☠ ☠ ☠ ☠

Unless you know what you're doing, and you have excellent timing, this is strictly for those who have plenty of disposable cash.

❐ 527. Buy jewelry.

☠ ☠ ☠

Here again, training plays a significant part in the transaction: if you're not trained, you have absolutely no idea what you're buying.

❏ 528. Buy jewelry as a gift.

☠ ☠ ☠

You might think this is the safest fallback position, gift-wise, especially if you're purchasing something for a female of the species, but that's certainly not the case. Everyone has their own taste, and very frequently yours and theirs does not dovetail in a complementary fashion. Besides, if you buy something the intended recipient does not normally wear—say, a big-ass pinkie ring—then they may feel grudgingly obligated to wear it whenever they see you, which is annoying.

❏ 529. Buy a diamond.

☠ ☠ ☠

Admit it: You have no clue what you're doing. Nobody does. A diamond is a rock someone finds in the ground, artificially enhanced in monetary value by systematic limitation of supply. Sure, diamonds have certain physical properties that make them useful for industrial or scientific endeavors, buy how often are you going to purchase a diamond so that you can increase your potential for manufacturing abrasives?

❏ 530. Buy a diamond as a gift.

☠ ☠ ☠ ☠

You can only fail here. Odds are, the recipient knows much more about diamonds than you do, and, therefore, exactly how much you paid. Worse, you got ripped off, and they underestimate what you paid, making you look not just like a dumbass, but a cheap dumbass.

❏ 531. Join a union.

☠ ☠ ☠

Give up your individual right to create your own contract, reduce your worth to that of your lowest colleague, and start paying dues.

❏ 532. Search for lost treasure.

☠ ☠ ☠ ☠

There's supposedly a whole bunch of it out there. All you have to do is find it. Of course, if it were really easy, someone would have already picked it up. Which would mean it wouldn't be "lost" anymore. There's a reason it's stayed lost this long. You can go broke trying to get rich.

❏ 533. Salvage lost treasure.

Even after you find it, you've still got to get it, and keep someone else from taking it.

☠ ☠ ☠ ☠

POLITICAL THINGS

In the United States, we have a participatory government, which means that old people vote religiously, and a certain minority of goofballs, groomed from youth or with a megalomaniacal bent, run for all offices. But that shouldn't stop you—jump right in!

❏ 534. Sign a petition allowing someone to run for public office, even though you would never want them elected, would never vote

for them, and find their politics personally distasteful.

This is what democracy is all about—a public forum for differing opinions, where anyone can stand up and be considered for the mantle of public office, even if that individual believes that tiny people living in the hood ornament of his car told him that the static between channels on his television set is a mind control device created by ancient Mayans.

❏ 535. Attend a public demonstration of some sort.

Remember the old saying, "Politics makes for strange bedfellows." Go to any demonstration, any public protest against anything—any cause, any activity, any person, any group. Doesn't matter which. Walk around. See people yelling and waving signs. Look at all the other people voicing their opinions for their own causes (either allied with or opposed to the main demonstration). Watch just how much goofier those tertiary groups become, as you move out toward the fringes. Strange bedfellows, indeed.

❏ 536. Vote for a candidate who has no possible way of winning whatsoever.

This is the American Way. Sure, anybody can pick a candidate who is probably going to win—what's the point of having democracy if you don't push the limits?

PART 1 PUBLIC THINGS

537. Start your own political party.

☠ ☠ ☠ ☠

There's a history of outstanding Americans who have decided that the mainstream groups just aren't meeting their needs, so they went out and started their own. Such as the founders of this country. Or, Mark Twain, who was a proud Mugwump. Use these icons as heroes, and go for it.

538. Join a political party that is not one of the "Big Two."

☠

Maybe you don't really want to start your political party; maybe that sounds like too much work. No big deal—there are plenty from which to choose. Did you know the American Communist Party is still around? They even have a Web site: *www.cpusa.org.*

539. Run for public office.

☠ ☠ ☠

You don't have to shoot for the brass ring or anything—hold off announcing your candidacy for the presidency. Start small, like running for chief of the local water district or something. You'd be surprised how many votes you get just for being on the ballot.

540. Renounce your citizenship.

☠ ☠ ☠ ☠

A potentially painful means of political protest.

❒ 541. Emigrate from your homeland.
💀 💀 💀 💀

For whatever reason, you don't like the place where you were born. So now you've got to pick somewhere else to live. Not the simplest of procedures, but getting easier as technology evolves.

❒ 542. Ask another nation for asylum.
💀 💀 💀 💀

Not only don't you want to live in the place you're from, but they would really like to hurt you if you went back. This is an advanced form of guilt-tripping someone into a gesture of pity, and a pretty important one, at that.

ARTISTIC THINGS

Creative accomplishment is pretty much a human endeavor; there are the odd apes or elephants who do some painting, and a few chimps with acting careers, and the vast majority of Web site design is performed by lemurs, but that's about all the animal kingdom contributes to the world's artistic collection. So be a proud member of your species: Do something creative. It's your birthright.

❒ 543. Write a book.
💀 💀

Stringing a bunch of words together is not nearly as difficult as writers would have you think. Stringing a bunch of words together that are worth reading, on the other hand, takes some diligence and patience.

544. Write a book of 1,001 things.

Include "writing a book of 1,001 things" as an entry.

545. Tell a joke.

This is not easy. There are many, many ways to screw up a joke, and really only a couple to tell it well and get a laugh.

546. Participate in an open-mic night at a comedy club and bomb.

It's a miserable, excruciating experience. There is nothing quite like it. Veteran comedians, people whose job it is to make other people laugh on command, dread this every moment of their lives (including when they sleep, during which time they dream about it).

547. Participate in improvisational comedy.

Much, much more difficult than performing comedy (which, in itself, is a bitter challenge).

548. Participate in competitive improvisational comedy.

Oddly enough, this is a bit easier than going it alone: It's a matter of practice, but you can learn to play off the other members of either team.

❏ 549. Write a play.
☠ ☠ ☠

What's so interesting about a few people standing around and yakking? Well, that's what you have to figure out. Unlike a movie, there's no padding a play with some action, like a car chase or a gun battle. Think it out, and rack your brain trying to get your characters to say something worth listening to.

❏ 550. Audition for a play.
☠ ☠

You don't have to actually get the part, but trying out is an excellent exercise in humility and bravado. Go for it. It can be a lot of fun. No kidding.

❏ 551. Act in a play in public.
☠ ☠ ☠

Pretending to be somebody else can be very rewarding—and pretending to be somebody else who is really unlike you can be really difficult and humiliating. Doing it in front of strangers is all of that.

❏ 552. Learn an exotic dance.
☠ ☠ ☠

There are myriad forms of rhythmic, physical forms of self-expression; some are kooky, some are painful and challenging, and some are downright sexy. Pick something you can use to show off. Tango, rumba, hip-hop, waltz, ballet, flamenco, polka, tap, even the Charleston.

☐ **553. Dance in public.**

☠ ☠ ☠

You'll never look as goofy as you think you look. Really. Just jumping up and kicking out the jams is extremely liberating, and even those who deride you will be totally jealous of your ability to let it all hang out.

☐ **554. Sing in public.**

☠ ☠

Yes, you really do sound silly. Unlike dancing, you can't possibly sound as good as you think you do. Still, your audience will be forgiving, because this takes a great deal of courage—unless you're charging admission, in which case they will be brutally critical.

☐ **555. Cut a record.**

☠ ☠ ☠

You think your music is so good that other people will pay to have their very own copy of it. Granted "cuttting" a "record" is kind of an archaic way of denoting this activity, but it's got the cachet of historical notoriety. Knock yourself out.

☐ **556. Paint a full-sized painting on canvas.**

☠

You might reveal that nascent talent, that sliver of disguised promise, that makes you the next Rembrandt. The worst possible result is that you will destroy some canvas by painting something so startlingly bad that your pets will go into seizures from looking at it.

❒ 557. Try to sell your art.
☠ ☠ ☠

Just because your efforts may have cost you a great deal of money and time, and might have great sentimental value for you, this does not mean that anyone else will place any value whatsoever on your work.

❒ 558. Carve a figurine out of a piece of wood.
☠ ☠ ☠

This is far more physically dangerous than most of the other artistic Things; we're talking loss of limb here. There's that old chestnut about removing the excess material from a raw hunk of medium to reveal the inner art—yeah, whatever. Big hint: Cut away from yourself. Gangrene is not pleasant. Keep a lot of antiseptic on hand.

❒ 559. Completely prep, paint, and assemble a miniature model car (the kind that requires you to shave off the nubs with an Xacto knife—not the kind that snaps together).
☠ ☠

Many young Americans go through this infuriating rite of passage—making a model of something, usually a vehicle, and usually a car. It looks really cool on the box, doesn't it? Yes, it does. For yours to look like that, you will part with many, many hours of your life, and possibly glue one part of your anatomy to another, and get really ripped on the fumes. It probably won't ever look as cool as the one on the box, either.

560. Participate in a radio broadcast.
☠ ☠

Let people hear what you have to say. . . . Odds are, it's pretty boring, but no less boring than whatever else happens to be on the radio. If you really want to be daring, do a live broadcast. Be sure to get a tape of the program, because, yes, you really do sound like that.

561. Try to win a contest sponsored by a radio station.
☠ ☠

I've done this, mostly when I was a kid. I was successful a couple times, too. Most recently, while writing this silly book, I stumped movie guy Jeff Howard with a question about the film *Miller's Crossing.* I rock.

562. Participate in a television broadcast.
☠ ☠ ☠

Now you can know what you really look and sound like. There's plenty of junk on television already, so no matter how lame your appearance turns out to be, you will definitely be better than most of the stuff on prime time. Try not to think about all those people staring at you, some of whom will have sick fantasies about you no matter how unattractive you are.

563. Participate in a live television broadcast.
☠ ☠ ☠ ☠

You have no idea what stupid thing you might say or do—which increases your nervousness, which increases the chances of you saying or doing something stupid, ad infinitum.

☐ 564. Try out for a television game show.

☠ ☠ ☠

You can't possibly be as stupid as most of the people who participate in those things. Unfortunately, you probably have too much personality.

☐ 565. Take a crack at a piñata.

☠

Beating something with a stick—few things can compare to the satisfaction this promises. Especially since you don't have to feel bad about it. You're beating an inanimate object. With candy inside. Yum!

Get pierced . . .
☐ 566. . . . through your ear.

☠

Way to go—you're now one gold hoop away from looking like a pirate.

☐ 567. . . . through both ears.

☠

Some people do this to children under the age of six, and it's legal. Yes, we, as a society, have decided that taking a needle and permanently mutilating your child is A-okay, but slapping them is not. Go figure.

❑ 568. . . . through your nose.

What happens when you get a cold?

❑ 569. . . . through your navel.

I am puzzled as to who came up with this particular type of adornment, and why. What were they thinking? "Oh, we need another place in the body in which to stab holes and put a sparkly thing—how 'bout the belly button?" That is definitely thinking outside the box. Coming up with the idea, that is. Doing it now is just copying a dumb trend, not original thought.

❑ 570. . . . through your lip.

Want to really spook everyone you meet? Introduce yourself with a safety pin poking through the very aperture you use to communicate.

❑ 571. . . . through your eyebrow.

The injury-to-eye motif has been around in literature for quite a while; there are few things more universally disturbing than a wound made to or near the eyeball. And now you're going to go and do that to yourself, of your own volition.

❒ 572.... through your tongue.

Mumph—mm—mmMumph. Mumphly-mumph. Mumphilly, mm—Mumph. No, really, what did you just say?

❒ 573.... through your nipple.

When I was growing up, one of the most abusive means of torturing your siblings and contemporaries was the "titty twister," whereby the antagonist grabbed the nipple of the victim, yanked, and put sufficient torque on the anatomy to cause incapacitating pain. Nowadays, instead of a demeaning attack on the unwary among your age demographic, it is a fashion trend.

❒ 574.... through your genitalia.

You're—going to—do what? To what? No, really—really? Uhhh ... okay. I guess. I mean—wait—really? No foolin'? Um ... how come? I mean ... no—wait. Really?

❒ 575.... through whatever else you can think of.

Because, gosh, ritual self-mutilation, in a vain attempt at self-aggrandizement by capturing the Zeitgeist (although, in actuality, you're captured by it, instead) is not enough, in terms of zones already navigated by those who have come before. No—you must break new ground. 'Cause, like, you'll show us what being a real rebel is all about. Bully for you.

576. Get a tattoo.

What possible thing could you put on your body that you'd want to see thirty years from now? No—stop and think about it for a second. Remember what you looked like/thought/said ten years ago? Was that person smart or talented or wonderful in any way? What makes you think that the person ten years from now is going to feel any different about you? But hey, maybe you'll receive the joy of hepatitis.

577. Get a tattoo that's visible to strangers.

Advertise your desire for self-mutilation; people are sure to make snap judgments about the kind of person you are.

578. Get a tattoo on your face.

Unless it's part of your tribal ritual, or you belong to a Maori culture, it's going to be difficult to justify this amendment of your features. Plus, head wounds bleed a lot. But hey, maybe you can offer your face for marketing purposes—it's worked before.

579. Be an extra in a feature film.

They're always looking for people—all kinds of people. You don't necessarily have to be attractive or in shape. This mostly involves a lot of standing around, taking conflicting direction from various crew members, and fighting oodles of boredom.

1001 THINGS TO DO IF YOU DARE

170

580. Make your own movie.

☠ ☠ ☠

No—home movies of your cute family and pets and silly friends do not count. We're talking about a real movie, with a plot, characters, and conflict. The technology is now ubiquitous, so you have no real excuse not to give it a go. Remember coming out of the theater thinking, "Boy, that sucked"? Well, demonstrate how you can do it better.

581. Memorize a poem.

☠ ☠

You'd be surprised how often something like that would come in handy. And if you're going to do it, do it right, don't pick something from Ogden Nash—get a good Poe or Kipling under your belt. Make it worthwhile.

582. Engage in a poetry slam competition.

☠ ☠

These people are not here to play. They are not adherents of the "roses are red" school of literature. They are extremely serious, and they have a strident point to get across. And they are pretty damned tough.

583. Attend an artistic display performed entirely by children.

☠ ☠ ☠ ☠

There are few things quite as grueling than a mass of untalented, youthful amateurs trying to engage in artistic expression.

❏ 584. Invent something.

☠ ☠ ☠

Be sure to get it patented (at the United States Patent and Trademark Office, of course: *www.uspto.gov*). If it's useful, hey, so much the better. Try to bear this in mind: Almost everything worth doing has been done already; just about everyone thinks they have a great idea, but very few really do.

❏ 585. Complete a crossword puzzle.

☠ – ☠ ☠, depending on difficulty

Learn a language well enough to satisfy the maddening cross-hatch of empty boxes by filling them with the appropriate letters. Start with something fairly easy, then work up to those monstrous, gargantuan complexities with hundreds of short-short clues. Five Down, "bird of myth," is "roc."

❏ 586. Complete the crossword puzzle in the Sunday edition of the "New York Times."

☠ ☠ ☠

Better linguists than you or I have tried and failed. This is the big one. Go for it. Set yourself a time limit, or face the possibility of going slightly mad.

❏ 587. Make your own clothing.

☠ – ☠ ☠, depending on circumstances

The means for accomplishing this are almost limitless: weaving, knitting, sewing, baking (if you really want to be daring). But creating the actual garments themselves is not the apex of the Thing—wearing them in public is.

588. Demolish a structure.

☠ – ☠ ☠ ☠ ☠ ☠, depending on conditions

For some reason, destroying something is immensely enjoyable—more enjoyable, even, than creating something. Maybe it's because the former doesn't usually involve as much attention to detail and planning. Unless, of course, your method of choice for demolition is explosives to cause an implosion.

589. Photograph a wild animal in its natural habitat.

☠ – ☠ ☠ ☠ ☠ ☠, depending on circumstances

Don't just pick a bunny rabbit or squirrel or something—for daring, stalk and shoot a panther or bear or hippo (on film). If you want a real challenge, and have the guts, don't use a telephoto lens. You can forgo asking your subjects to yell "Cheese."

590. Photograph someone who really doesn't want his or her photo taken.

☠ ☠ ☠ ☠

A mobster in court. A pillar of the community caught sexing up a sheep. These people will do all sorts of things to keep from appearing on film. Laugh at them.

591. Learn to throw your voice.

☠

The much-maligned art of ventriloquism suffers from an image problem, probably as a result of all those evil, alcoholic, murderous ventriloquists. But just think of how many times being able to talk while you're drinking a glass of water will come in handy!

592. Learn some magic.

This doesn't have to be sawing your partner in half, or surviving a dunk tank while in a straitjacket or anything. You can learn a couple of little party tricks involving a deck of playing cards or coins or something. It's always nice to have something that will startle or amaze people, as long as it isn't too lame.

593. Learn to eat fire.

Okay, so you're not actually eating fire. Instead, you use a combination of hand-eye coordination and the laws of physics. Anyone—even you—can eat fire. Of course, safety precautions are necessary (as with any use of fire), and a high pain threshold is desirable, as you will inevitably suffer burns to the lips, tongue, mouth, and throat. For more info, visit the Web site of the North American Fire Arts Association: *www.nafaa.org.*

594. Perform some taxidermy.

This is all about stuffing an animal, and I don't mean with breading. Usually, this is a practice seen as creepy and asocial, reserved for the likes of Norman Bates and his alleged model, Ed Gein. Playing with dead animals can elicit this type of reaction, but so what? Who are you trying to impress? Get out your needle and thread and get to work!

❏ 595. Write a news article.

☠ ☠ ☠

Sure, it can't be that hard—look at the people who do it. But actually doing it in a way that's somewhat accurate, getting all that information in the correct order, with a coherent narrative, and not inventing bits and pieces, well, that's pretty tough. Avoiding the response from your readers is not so easy, either.

❏ 596. Learn to play a musical instrument.

☠ ☠ ☠

It's not just about hand-eye coordination. It's not just about patience. It's not just about a natural inclination and talent for such things. It's about all of that, and more.

❏ 597. Tag something with spray paint.

☠ ☠

Some call this vandalism; the authorities treat it as such—even when simultaneously taking your stolen tax dollars to finance ludicrous and crappy "public art." Go out and create your own public art, using the wonderful invention of paint in a pressurized can. Be creative—"Leonard Loves Micki" does not cut it. Oh, and it's illegal. So maybe you shouldn't.

❏ 598. Throw and fire a clay pot.

☠

Get it to turn out like you intended it to. The former is pretty easy—almost every third-grader has access to a kiln of some sort and has created some pretty miserable works of "art" (the status to which they are relegated, because it's obvious they can't have any utilitarian function whatsoever). It's the latter that's hard—making a drinking mug when you mean to make a drinking mug, or a bowl that's bowl-shaped and will hold liquid. Something that survives the process, despite your utter incompetence.

❏ 599. Fell a tree with an ax.
☠ ☠

The tree is actually pretty good at sustaining a lot of damage—that's what it was bred to do. That's why there are still trees on this planet. It's going to take you a lot of chopping to pull this off, even for a skinny tree. You go, Paul Bunyan.

❏ 600. Fell a tree with a chainsaw.
☠ ☠

Okay, now we're talking. There's something about an engine you can hold in your hands, especially if it's powering a device with the destructive power offered by a chainsaw. Slicing wood with a chainsaw isn't like work—it's more like playtime for grown-ups. Even after you chop down the tree, then chop it up into manageable pieces, you're still going to want to do some more chopping. If you can swing it, take one of those old pieces of furniture you've been meaning to get rid of and . . .

❏ 601. Slice up a piece of furniture with a chainsaw.
☠ ☠ ☠

There's really nothing like it. Talk about fun! Be sure to wear gloves and goggles and all that safety shiznat—nails and springs and other furniturey-type stuff is going to come flying out at the equivalent of 275 miles per hour.

602. Trim a tree, with a chainsaw, while perched in its branches.

☠ ☠ ☠ ☠

Up there, you might tend to forget that you've got to concentrate not only on the current location of the spinning chain, but also on your feet, and their relation to the branch they are supported by, and that branch's dependence on other branches. . . . You don't want to cut the wrong one, for sure. Bear that in mind. Also, best not to use an electric chainsaw—you don't want to worry about where the cord is while you're focusing on all that other stuff.

603. Light off fireworks.

☠

There are few things more archetypically American than causing explosions for no particular reason. Fireworks are just miniature explosives, manufactured in bulk, and quality-controlled for safety in home usage. Theoretically.

604. Light fireworks in your hand.

☠ ☠

While fireworks are generally designed and produced with safety in mind, there are some pretty basic safety requirements associated with deploying them. Probably the first of these is: Don't hold it in your hand when you light it. For thirty-five cents apiece, do you really think each fuse is a perfectly honed instrument of timing? And no, sparklers don't count. According to the CDC, 9,300 Americans were treated for fireworks-related injuries in 2003. Four of them died.

❐ 605. Hop a fence.

☠

There's the always-cool one-handed vault over the top, usually performed on a waist-high wooden-panel demarcation, or the two-handed press-up-and-swing-legs-over means of traversing a wall of chest height. However you do it, know that you gotta come down on the other side. . . . Try to know what's on the other side first.

❐ 606. Hop a fence lined with barbed wire.

☠ ☠

Usually found on farms or wooded lots, this can be found in single- or multiple-strand configurations. The trick is to get over all the wire without getting hung up on barbs. Not too difficult for crafty humans; this is mainly to keep livestock in one place, and to keep them from getting ideas.

❐ 607. Hop a fence topped with razor tape.

☠ ☠ ☠

This stuff is nasty: strands of wire with no-kidding stainless-steel razors embedded every few inches; this can really ruin your day. Odds are, whoever put this up wants to keep you out.

❏ 608. Hop a fence topped with concertina wire.

☠ ☠ ☠ ☠

This can be either barbed wire or razor tape, wound in big loops, like an evil extended Slinky. Common knowledge suggests that throwing a jacket or blanket over the wire will allow you to traverse it safely; this is true, but only if the jacket or blanket is made out of Kevlar. Better just to avoid it entirely. Hey, it's your flesh. Make sure your tetanus shots are up to date.

❏ 609. Build a fence.

☠ ☠

It is said that they make good neighbors. That's probably not inaccurate. Of course, it's also easier said than done: a good fence has to be sturdy, and survive the elemental forces. You usually have to dig down into the ground, and really get the components placed properly. Not easy work.

❏ 610. Build a barbed-wire fence.

☠ ☠ ☠

It's getting the postholes dug that's the tough part. And you have to be careful not to stab yourself repeatedly when stringing the wire. This is a painfully funny sitcom moment waiting to happen—not so funny if it happens to you, though.

❏ 611. Build a wooden fence.

☠ ☠ ☠

Probably not a one-person job. You have to position the slats so you can attach them to the posts. Not easy solo.

612. Build a stone wall.
☠ ☠ ☠ ☠

If a fence is tough, then a stone wall is the epitome of "back-breaking work." Lift with your legs. And don't drop one on your foot.

613. Learn to say "f--- you" in forty languages, one of which is spoken only in a small village in Africa.
☠ ☠

Communication is about getting your point across. "F--- you" is about the most basic point imaginable. Besides, it's also incredibly flexible—with the proper intonation, inflection, and delivery, it can mean almost anything.

614. Build your own Web site.
☠ ☠

HTML. JavaScript. Perl. Whatever. You got something to say, in today's world, you say it online. And the really gutsy ones go and figure out how to do it for themselves, instead of letting someone else do the hosting and design.

615. Try to make money off a Web site.
☠ ☠

Yeah, there was a time when they were giving money to anyone who could even spell "dot-com," but that time has long passed. And that's not necessarily a bad thing; you now have to have both a viable idea and a means to execute it before you can make money on the Internet. It's darned tough, even then.

❏ **616. Watch a foreign film.**

☠

Foreigners do not think like us—that is what makes them foreign. Because of this, you will notice that foreign films often contain plot points, situations, and characters which make no sense to you, the viewer, whatsoever, but which the director assumed everyone would understand. This is probably why they're always called "foreign films" instead of "foreign movies."

❏ **617. Watch an old, black-and-white, foreign film, with subtitles.**

☠ ☠ ☠

You don't have to necessarily pretend it has artistic merit; just watch it to see if it's worth watching.

❏ **618. Perform any feat mentioned in a Warren Zevon song.**

☠ – ☠ ☠ ☠ ☠ ☠, depending on choice

Jungle fighter. Envoy. Freelance writer. Werewolf. There are a plethora of zany activities suggested by the man, and they're all just waiting for your level-best attempt.

❏ **619. Make an igloo.**

☠

You'd be surprised how easy it is. Well, how easy it is to build one that stays up for a little while. Use that good, wet, heavy packing snow. Sleep in it overnight.

PART 1 PUBLIC THINGS

❏ 620. Wait backstage after a performance to meet the performer.

☠ ☠

Get an autograph, shake their hand. Flattering for them, transcendent for you. But don't overstay your welcome: be polite, get the autograph, shake their hand, tell them how great they are, thank them, and get the hell out.

❏ 621. Learn to be a sword-swallower.

☠ ☠ ☠ ☠ ☠

Yeah, take a long, sharp metal object and shove it down your throat. Sounds like a recipe for disaster, doesn't it? It does. And probably is. So be damned careful when going about the instructional process, and be sure not to leave a copy of this book around where someone might trip over it while trying to get you some medical attention.

❏ 622. Engage in a form of self-immolation, either to protest something, or as a form of religious expression.

☠ ☠ ☠ ☠ ☠

Er . . . this is pretty impressive, all right. I mean, a human being burning is the kind of thing that people stop to look at. Of course, you can usually only do this once.

❏ 623. Attempt satire.

☠ ☠ ☠

Sure, it looks easy—even seeming idiots pull it off, time and again. What many folks don't realize is that those apparent idiots are actually extremely talented individuals, even using simplistic mechanisms to deliver clever humor. Try it one time and see: you'll be amazed how many people don't get the joke—and the joke, like all things, will be dead after the autopsy, if it hasn't expired before it.

☐ 624. Read a sample of someone else's writing.
☠ ☠ ☠

There are very few people who can put together ideas in a coherent manner, using the written word. There are, unfortunately, many, many, many more who think they can.

☐ 625. Read someone else's unedited, unpublished book.
☠ ☠ ☠

Okay, for as few people there are that can string an idea out onto a page, using words instead of cartoons, there are even fewer who can do it at book length. While publishing may be an incestuous, backbiting, nasty, artificial little business, it at least serves the purpose of keeping most of the really crappy stuff away from an unsuspecting public. Sure, some lousy books get published—but you should see the truly crummy stuff that never makes it off the publisher's desk. . . .

☐ 626. Listen to another culture's music.
☠ ☠

Strangely, music is an art that is often particularly geared to a specific culture, at a specific time in history. Sure, there are certain tunes, melodies, and whatnot that can transcend time

PART 1 PUBLIC THINGS

183

and populace, but those seem to be the exceptions, not the rule. Even more so than film, music can please a certain ear, and scrape against those not receptive to it.

❏ 627. Listen to an hour of music that originated in Southwest Asia.
☠ ☠ ☠

For many Westerners, this particular type of sound is the audio equivalent of puncturing your genitals with an awl, then soaking them in bleach. Bengali, Indian, Pakistani . . . doesn't matter.

❏ 628. Listen to an hour of music that originated in the Mediterranean.
☠ ☠ ☠

The bouzouki is a device that seems purposefully intended to molest the tiny bones inside your inner ear. Unless, of course, you are Mediterranean, both genetically and culturally. In which case, you have probably built up a tolerance, but most likely still don't enjoy it all that much.

❏ 629. Listen to an hour of music that was written over a hundred years ago.
☠

Classical music or opera accompanied by a Bugs Bunny cartoon does not count.

❏ 630. Listen to an hour of pop music written twenty or more years after you were born.
☠ ☠ ☠

This is not meant for you to enjoy. In fact, if done properly, it is specifically designed to annoy the living piss out of you; if it doesn't, then the current generation has absolutely no creativity, or culture to call their own. Losers.

❒ 631. Listen to an hour of freeform jazz riffs.
☠ ☠ ☠
You may love this. On the other hand, the rhythmless, disordered, anarchic sounds may assault your brain viciously, battering it into a pulpy mess.

Bathe a . . .
❒ 632. . . . pet dog.
☠ – ☠ ☠ ☠ ☠, depending on circumstances
The difficulty of this really depends on the specific breed. Some dogs actually dig it. But, whether you've got a dog that is into bathing or not, you should prepare to get wet.

❒ 633. . . . pet cat.
☠ ☠ ☠
Unlike dogs, who can go either way in about a fifty-fifty split, cats are just about uniform in their dislike of being wet. Probably because they know how silly they look when soaked. You've never seen your cat fight until you've tried to dunk it.

❒ 634. . . . pet snake.
☠ ☠ ☠
I guess some snakes, such as the cottonmouth or anaconda, are big fans of water—they spend a lot of time there. But try, for

instance, a boa constrictor in the bathtub, and see how possible it is for an animal with no legs to climb a tile wall.

❑ 635. . . . domesticated horse.
☠ ☠

It's not exactly a tough job, but it's a big job. Wears on the upper arms, it does.

❑ 636. . . . wild animal, of any type.
☠ ☠ ☠ ☠

Not quite sure why you'd want to do this, but I imagine it would be really tricky. Because—the animal won't like it.

❑ 637. Shoe a horse.
☠ ☠ ☠ ☠

There's an art to smithing, which made it such a widespread trade back when horses were the preferred mode of trans-portation. Plus, horses need shoes. They are not exactly fond, however, of misplaced nails that strike the sensitive part of the hoof, and they are not at all forgiving of dumbassed humans.

❑ 638. Clean a horse's hooves.
☠ ☠ ☠

There's a specific tool for this, called the "hoof pick," or "hoof knife," or "hoof scraper," or "hoof thingy." The deal is that the horse's hooves get full of gunk, and need to be cleaned out. Even the horse understands this. Still, the animal is probably not thrilled when you poke and prod at what are basically its toenails—especially if you jam a metal implement into the wrong piece of its hoof. (Ever cut the quick of your toenail by accident? same kind of pain, but bigger, because the horse is bigger.) And you don't want to piss off the horse. According to at least one report, 50,000 Americans are treated for horse-related injuries in a given year, and 40 percent of those were due to kicks.

❒ 639. Go on tour.
☠ ☠ ☠

So your artistic gig is pleasing to enough people that you think you can hack it on the circuit? Well then, get out there! Stay in those hotels, eat that convention food, and do some hand exercises (for signing autographs, of course).

❒ 640. Build some furniture.
☠ ☠

Unlike other crafts, furniture is meant to be used. You're going to sit on it, or lie down on it, or put socks inside it, and it's going to have to be built well enough to provide whatever service you intended. So you're providing yourself with inherent risk. Cool.

❒ 641. Re-enact a scene from your favorite film.
☠ ☠ ☠

Try to refrain from comments about life imitating art, okay? It's sometimes a hoot to ape something you've always admired. Try to be cool about this, though—refrain if the movie you had in mind features zombies in prominent roles, or a scene in which the bank teller goes down on the pizza delivery guy.

642. Go to Tiffany's in Manhattan, equipped with a tin ring and $50 (allowing for inflation).

☠ ☠ ☠ ☠

If you don't know the rest, you need to watch more movies.

643. Create your own porn.

☠ ☠ ☠ ☠

Stills or full-motion video, whatever kind of stuff you want. Today it's easy, with digital cameras, InterCyberWeb. . . . Back in the day, you had to take the 110 to the Photomat, and trust the people inside.

644. Trust your significant other to hold onto the homemade porn.

☠ ☠ ☠ ☠ ☠

Sure, and right after that, give your lover the key to the safety deposit box, access to your firearms, and a medical power of attorney. Homemade porn is one of those things that is never destroyed, never goes away, is never lost—although it may be found by strangers—and has amazing transitional properties. They should make the space shuttle out of the stuff.

645. Write your name in wet cement.

☠

Optimally, this will be wet cement that you own, so as not to infringe on someone else's wet cement. It's a lame attempt at immortality but, for some of us, it's the best chance we've got. Make it as big as possible.

TRAVEL THINGS

It's been suggested that the vast majority of individuals die within twelve miles of where they were born . . . without ever having left the immediate geophysical region during the interim. This, to me, is just sad: The planet is pretty big, and spending your entire life in one tiny corner of it seems like a lot of wasted opportunity. Get out of town—go explore, go see what's to see. Maybe you won't even like it elsewhere . . . but at least you'll die knowing you're happy with the place where you chose to die.

❏ 646. Travel to a foreign country.
☠

Any country. Nothing will make you appreciate home quite as much as spending time elsewhere.

❏ 647. Travel to a foreign country where they don't speak English.
☠ ☠ ☠

Yeah, that language barrier is a lot more daunting when you're faced with something more than just ordering a meal in an ethnic restaurant. You now have to get by on your mime abilities and patience.

❏ 648. Travel to a foreign country where they don't speak English and they hate Americans.
☠ ☠ ☠

This isn't cute, it isn't fun, and it poses a real, constant danger. Be very, very careful. For increased safety, pretend to be Canadian.

❏ 649. Travel to a foreign city under siege from terrorism.

☠ ☠ ☠ ☠

Terrorists are not bright people. That's one of the reasons they're terrorists—smart people don't grow up to choose "terrorizing others" as a job description, because there's not a big future in it. So foreign terrorists, by and large, think you are personally responsible for every ill our nation has perpetrated globally, we are all agents working for our government, and that we have wealthy families prepared to offer exorbitant ransoms for our safe return.

❏ 650. Travel to a foreign city under siege by its own military.

☠ ☠ ☠ ☠ ☠

Thugs don't scare me—the most they're going to want from me is my wallet. Terrorists are scarier, but it's often possible to negotiate with terrorists. A nineteen-year-old with a uniform, a gun, and a purpose—now that's really scary.

❏ 651. Backpack across a continent.

☠ ☠ ☠

Pick a small one, like Europe, where there are plenty of places to buy water and snacks. Europe also has hostels; hostel means "place where unkempt backpackers sleep and are robbed" in European.

1001 THINGS TO DO IF YOU **DARE**

❏ 652. Visit all seven continents.

☠ ☠ ☠ ☠

Antarctica is the really tricky one—you have to get permission, and/or have a pretty good reason to go there.

❏ 653. Go into the wilderness.

☠ – ☠ ☠ ☠ ☠ ☠, depending on locale

To those raised ensconced in concrete and steel, some trees, grass, and lots of stars can look awfully damned spooky. But it's really not all that bad; there are few things left that can kill you outright. In the American wilderness, anyway. Wilderness in another country like, say, Asia? You're dead.

❏ 654. Spend New Year's Eve in Times Square.

☠ ☠ ☠

There are actually very few places where the word *throngs* is accurate and applicable in literature. It's a word often abused, as a way of saying "crowds" without sounding so pedestrian. Well, on New Year's Eve, in Times Square, you can safely use that word without fear of misusing it.

❏ 655. Spend New Year's Eve on the Vegas Strip.

☠ ☠ ☠

Vegas is usually pretty crowded on any given day. On New Year's Eve, goofballs from all over the planet find it somehow pleasurable to congregate on the street outside the larger casinos and wander around drinking.

❏ 656. Spend Fat Tuesday in New Orleans.

☠ ☠ ☠

Again, there seems to be some mystique in clustering with like-minded bumblef---s whom you don't know, for the express purpose of imbibing alcohol and walking up and down the street.

❏ 657. Visit Rio for Carnival.

☠ ☠ ☠

Carnival is not just about walking around and drinking; it's about walking around, drinking, dancing, and sex. Which seems a lot more interesting.

❏ 658. Spend spring break wherever the kids happen to be spending it this year.

☠ ☠

There have been many "hot" places for the traditional spring break gatherings over the years: Daytona, Fort Lauderdale, Lake Havasu, South Padre, Cancun, Scranton. . . . All the North American hotspots have been tapped at one time or another (and still are today). If you like being around a bunch of immature drunks, all of whom are busy getting drunk in immature fashion, and are bent on property damage and noise, this is the place for you.

❏ 659. Go on safari in the African veldt.

☠ ☠ ☠ ☠

There's some big, dangerous critters in that place. Really big, and really dangerous. Of course, the most dangerous African critters aren't big at all—it's the microscopic nasties that are so deadly. They got stuff that hasn't even been discovered yet, because whoever gets it just dies right there, so the sickness is never diagnosed. Be sure to get your shots first—as if that will help.

☐ 660. Go into the Australian bush.
☠ ☠ ☠

It's big. So big, there's parts of it that have never been seen, up close and personal, by anything other than a dingo or bird. Sure—Qantas flies over, and it's been mapped very well . . . but it's still fairly empty. Take a good deal of water, and some kind of tracking system (GPS, etc.).

☐ 661. Visit the Grand Canyon.
☠

Yes, it's just a big hole in the ground. Which is like saying an orgasm is just an itch being scratched. Better writers than I have described it—so I won't even try. Just go and do it, dammit.

☐ 662. See the northern or southern lights (aurora borealis or australis).
☠ ☠

Usually, you have go way up (or down) into some dreary polar latitudes to catch a glimpse of this phenomenon, but sometimes, not too often, conditions will be just right for you to see it from almost anywhere in the northern hemisphere.

☐ 663. See the Southern Cross.
☠ ☠

Not nearly as amazing as the northern/southern lights. It's just some stars in the sky, and you can pretty much see stars from wherever you are. But these stars are only visible from the Southern Hemisphere, so it's a good excuse to get down to the Southern Hemisphere. Nice.

🔲 664. Cross an international border illegally.
☠ ☠ ☠ ☠

There are really very few places in the world where the demarcation between one nation and another is clearly defined by any tangible symbol. Most borders are literally only lines on a map. So walk, drive, swim, or fly across one or two. It shouldn't be too difficult. I remind you: This is not legal. That means it's a crime.

🔲 665. Drive across the continental United States.
☠

We got us a big country here. It's full of really cool stuff. We also have the most extensive, complex, and well-maintained system of roads, streets, and highways on the planet. So exploit it— make the most of it, and get out there and hit the open road.

🔲 666. Drive across the continental United States, switching off with another driver, stopping only for gas, food, and bathroom breaks.
☠ ☠

See what kind of time you can make.

🔲 667. Drive from Frisco to L.A. on the Pacific Coast Highway.
☠

Call it what you will—everybody does. US 1. Cabrillo Highway.

Whatever. It's that long, gorgeous stretch of road that is on the left-most boundary of the continental United States. You want to go from north to south, because that way you'll be in the outside lane, looking right out over the water. Preferably in July, in a convertible. Then get out of California as fast as possible.

❏ 668. Drive Interstate 70, from Denver to Grand Junction.
☠ ☠

You get to go into the mountains, then through the mountains, then down out of the mountains. Scenery to make postcard manufacturers wet their collective pants. Try to time it right, though—blizzards often shut down the Eisenhower Tunnel in the winter. And traffic can really suck on the weekends. One more thing: Try to remember that every single stretch of road in the world is a potential falling-rock area; the ones with the signs are those places that have already proven to be falling-rock areas. Don't get cocky.

❏ 669. Drive from Denver to Frisco in thirty hours.
☠ ☠ ☠ ☠ ☠

In the tradition of one of the best of the classic chase films, this one is not easy with modern vehicles and laws.

❏ 670. Drive Highway 375 in Nevada.
☠ ☠

What the state now officially calls the "Extraterrestrial Highway," because, well, Nevadans have a wry, cynical side that is quite apt to co-opt any nonsensical goofiness and try to make a buck off it. Supposedly, there are some aliens flying around up there, on a mega-classified Air Force base. Yes. Uh-huh. And supposedly this book will make me a millionaire.

❏ 671. Swim in as many oceans/seas/lakes/ rivers/large bodies of water as possible.
☠ ☠ ☠

Check 'em off as you complete each. Start simple: each of the Great Lakes. Then try the oceans. Scatter your efforts as much as possible. Keep a list.

❏ 672. Take the train from coast to coast (your choice: either latitudinally or longitudinally).
☠ ☠ ☠ ☠

Expect frequent, long delays.

❏ 673. Ride the rails like a hobo.
☠ ☠ ☠ ☠ ☠

I'm not quite sure who the marketing genius was, that crafty clown who, over a hundred years ago, implanted in the collective American mind the idea that wandering the land, at the speed of train travel, was a romantic and nigh-regal concept. That person should get a medal from the Public Relations Flak Hall of Fame, if such a thing exists. The traditional fantastic motif involves a freight train with a flamboyant name, a topcoat, some fingerless gloves, and a stick holding a satchel made from a knotted kerchief. The real deal involves dirty, cramped conditions; slow, uncomfortable travel; and gang-rape at the hands of diseased vagrants.

❑ 674. Spend forty-eight hours in a major metropolitan center without a home or hotel.

☠ ☠ ☠

Think of it as an extended travel layover—but don't stay in your port of embarkation; get out and see the city. Walk around. Meet people. Eat in local dives. Drag your belongings with you from place to place. As you start to get really wired, when the lack of sleep starts to fuzz your mind and dawn is yet a few hours away, wander into a small, twenty-four-hour dining establishment of some sort. Make some infrequent, minor purchases until the sun comes back up, and do it again. Stagger into your place of departure on fumes, collapsing into a puddled heap once you finally reach your mode of transportation.

❑ 675. Smuggle something through customs.

☠ ☠ ☠

This was a lot more fun when we weren't so damned uptight about terrorism, in that brief lull between the highjacking trend in the '60s and '70s and the September 11 attacks. The security staff who work as customs personnel have become really twitchy in virtually every country on the planet. A sex toy in your luggage wouldn't just be something they smirk at nowadays.

❑ 676. Smuggle a pet through customs.

☠ ☠ ☠ ☠

A snake will think of you as a big, warm, soft tree (inasmuch as a snake can think, of course). So if you wrap it around your waist, under a bulky sweatshirt, it will stay nice and snug until you get to the other side of the customs area, where you can put it back in your carry-on luggage. No kidding.

☐ 677. Be a space tourist.
☠ ☠ ☠ ☠ ☠

Right now, flinging yourself into extra-atmospheric orbit is an extremely expensive proposition, and most of us are unable to avail ourselves of the opportunity. Very soon, though, this should be fairly practical, so why not make a point of accomplishing it.

☐ 678. Circumnavigate the globe.
☠ ☠ ☠ ☠ ☠

There are several different means to accomplish this: boat, airplane, even—theoretically—by balloon. It's never easy, and only a few people in all of history have accomplished it. Be sure to pack a lunch.

☐ 679. Walk across the downtown area of a major metropolitan city some time after midnight, and before 5 A.M.
☠ ☠ ☠

For some reason, crime and criminals like to congregate in the city center, under cover of darkness. I think this is because (a) that's where all the things and people worth robbing/stealing are located, and (b) nighttime is the traditional occasion for dirty deeds. Hanging out during this period, in this area, is a bad idea. Keep your wits about you.

680. Cross to the other side of town via the sewer system.

☠

It's been said that a good measure of any civilization is its capacity for removing human waste. By that criterion, America is one damned fine nation—we've got some bee-yoo-ti-ful sewers, and they span far and wide and deep. You can drop down into one without any specific tools or know-how, and wander around for days on end in the labyrinth they form. Bring some heavily scented cream for your upper lip.

681. Live in the Manhattan sewer system for a week.

☠ ☠ ☠ ☠

Supposedly, there are colonies of vagrants nestled down there, with an extensive warren of hidey-holes and a rudimentary society built from primitive gibberish. And crocodiles.

682. Visit the embassy of a foreign country.

☠

They might feed you exotic cuisine, native to the nation the embassy represents, such as falafel, dolmes, or Coca-Cola and potato chips. You may meet dignitaries, or embassy staffers, diplomats trained to communicate with Americans in our own peculiar mode of conversation (brash, loud, and overly personal).

683. Visit your own embassy while traveling abroad.

☠ ☠ ☠

Just leaving our country will make you appreciate it more. But going to one of our embassies while in a foreign country will let you see how much other people really appreciate our country, too. Even in a country with a government and population that purports to hate Americans, there is usually a long line of people waiting eagerly to get inside and make their pitch for a visa. One of the best feelings in the world, the warmest sort of camaraderie, is when those Marine guards wave you past the line and right inside because you have that blue (or green) passport with an eagle on the front of it.

684. Have sex in all fifty states.

☠ ☠ ☠

It's good to have goals. Plus, it's one great excuse to get out and see this country of ours. It can be, however, somewhat challenging to come up with reasons to go to some of our states. That's part of the fun, too.

685. Have sex with the same partner in all fifty states.

☠ ☠ ☠ ☠

Now you've doubled the complexity of the thing. Yowza.

686. Visit Barbados.

☠ ☠ ☠

Wicked-cool island paradise. The natives not only speak English, but they like Americans. That's a refreshing treat, to be sure. Very economical, incredibly gorgeous. Good snorkeling/diving, too, with some wrecks readily available right off the coast, placed there as artificial reefs. Beautiful.

❏ 687. Go to Colombia.

☠ ☠ ☠ ☠ ☠

Gorgeous land, friendly people, terrific food, great prices. In the words of my closest friend: "If they would just get their political act together, this would be a great tourist destination."

❏ 688. Hit Amsterdam.

☠ ☠ ☠

Yeah, there's the stuff with the Red Light District, and the drug bars, and the beer—but they also have . . . good food. The foreign restaurants, I mean. Dutch food pretty much sucks.

❏ 689. Visit Anne Frank's house.

☠ ☠ ☠

Okay, it's not really Anne's house; it's the house where she stayed while hiding from Nazis and writing her book. It's a powerful place to be—to see just where she was, and get a feel for the size of the place.

❏ 690. Go to the Middle East.

☠ ☠ ☠ ☠ ☠

See what all the shouting is about. Then leave as soon as possible.

❒ **691. Go to Israel.**

☠ ☠ ☠ ☠ ☠

A lot of people go to visit, for many reasons. On any given day, you risk not only the common dangers of any metropolitan area (mugging, stabbing, etc.), but also cars exploding, suicide bombers, and all other sorts of terrorist-related misery.

❒ **692. Go to Jerusalem.**

☠ ☠ ☠ ☠ ☠

See the city people are willing to kill and die for.

❒ **693. Go to Mecca.**

☠ ☠ ☠ ☠ ☠

Evidently, there are quite a few people who get a kick out of this. It's a pretty big deal for many folks. You might want to see what they're all talking about.

❒ **694. Go to Mecca during the pilgrimage.**

☠ ☠ ☠ ☠ ☠

Throngs of people, crowded together, sharing a religious experience. Sort of like New Orleans during Mardi Gras, without the alcohol, sex, or fun.

❒ **695. Visit England.**

☠ ☠

Sure, the weather is dreary and the food isn't exactly the height of fine cuisine, but the British are some fine folks, and they dig their revolutionary cousins. Plus, they all sound so smart, 'cause they've got that great accent.

❒ 696. Go to London.

☠ ☠

There's all the big-time touristy stuff. It's a bit expensive, but well worth seeing.

❒ 697. See a show in Piccadilly Circus.

☠ ☠ ☠

Home to world-renowned theater, and with good cause. Well worth the exorbitant price.

❒ 698. Visit Scotland.

☠ ☠ ☠

They tell me that Scotland is a whole separate country from England, but I can't for the life of me figure out how. Anyway, they have Scotch there. And Scots. Last time I was there, I almost got beat up by two skinheads—and I hadn't even made any jokes about men wearing skirts. Wait—that was in Carlisle. . . . Is that England or Scotland? Who can tell the difference?

❒ 699. Visit a no-kidding Scottish castle.

☠ ☠ ☠

Learn that castle life was probably not nearly as romantic as we like to think it was. Scratch that—it was definitely not even slightly romantic. And all that nonsense about who had what scepter, or where the actual crown was, and what royal ass was planted on which rock. . . . Very, very silly, to contemporary minds. But I guess they didn't have television back then, and needed something to talk about.

PART 1 PUBLIC THINGS

700. Drive a car in Great Britain.

☠ ☠ ☠ ☠ ☠

Pure, unadulterated misery. If you can't make it over to England, or get there and can't find a car, punch holes in your body with an awl, and that will approximate the same sensation.

701. Visit Japan.

☠ ☠ ☠

There is something absolutely infuriating about people who smile politely when they have no idea what you're trying to communicate to them. I think it has to do with an American inferiority complex, in that we think we're being laughed at, when we just really want to get to the bathroom. Daring not only for cultural shock, but the expense and distance.

702. Visit Tokyo.

☠ ☠ ☠ ☠

Okay, when I was looking for that Japanese bathroom, I finally found someone who was able to figure out what I needed. Blushing and smiling furiously (yes, the Japanese are a people who have the cultural adaptation to smile furiously), I was directed to a room that contained a chair that looked like a science-fiction device. Suffice it to say, learning what all the electronic buttons did, in an attempt to make the thing flush, was a discomfiting experience.

703. Stay in a hotel.

☠

It's a place that you don't own, usually comprised solely of a bedroom, where you get to sleep in exchange for a rental fee.

The place exists for just this purpose, which means others have stayed in the room before you, and others will stay in the room after you've left. Try not to think about what that means about the bedding. . . .

704. Stay in a crummy hotel.
☠ ☠ ☠

Surprisingly, the pay-by-the-hour, no-tell motels are not the biggest fleabags, in my experience. As a matter of fact, the worst place I ever stayed in was not a $15-per-hour room in the back streets of a metropolitan city, but a hotel that belongs to a major hotel chain, located in rural Indiana. The floor was matted with filth, the various amenity fixtures (such as lighting and heat) didn't work, and I was forced to kill not one but two crickets who had made themselves at home between the wall and the air conditioner. Not the best night's sleep on record.

705. Stay in a five-star hotel.
☠ ☠ ☠

True, the rooms may compare unfavorably with their $60-a-night counterparts, but they certainly rarely warrant a price tag six times that. What does make the difference (and what you're really paying for at these places) is the service, which is almost uniformly superb.

706. Stay at an all-inclusive resort.
☠ ☠ ☠

The kind of place where your payment covers not only your room, but food, and often some form of entertainment as well.

These are touted as the end-all, be-all of travel luxury, but can be close to a rip-off if you don't carefully inspect the value. Make sure your alcoholic beverages are included in the price, as that's where you're going to make up a lot of the differential in cost.

❏ 707. Go to the Artichoke Capital of the World.
☠☠☠☠

Castroville, California, sports a giant-ass artichoke, as well as a few restaurants that will dish up the best vegetable in the world in a maddeningly diverse array of forms, such as deep-fried, baked, and steamed, in unlikely dishes that include artichoke bread, artichoke soup, and—yes—even artichoke cake.

❏ 708. Visit Death Valley.
☠☠☠

This is one of the hottest, driest, lowest places on Earth (of course, it's in California, where hospitality is at a premium). Do not stay long. Heck, if you can swing it, don't even get out of your vehicle.

❏ 709. Drive through Death Valley during the springtime bloom.
☠☠☠

Strangely, if enough rain falls on the region during winter, an amazing amount and variety of wildflowers bloom in April or May. This is very impressive. Take lots of water.

710. Run the Badwater Ultramarathon.
☠ ☠ ☠ ☠ ☠

A 135-mile race through Death Valley. Criminal stupidity. These people should have been bred out of existence, through simple natural selection.

711. Do New York City.
☠ ☠ ☠ ☠

Thousands of years from now, historians will goggle at the complexity and vastness of the city rising from the tiny island and its outlying areas. They will mention it in reverent tones, eliciting the same reactions we currently feel when we hear the names "Thebes," "Troy," "Babylon," and "Atlantis." Granted, they will not have known how expensive, dirty, and full of New Yorkers it was, or how vastly overrated were its attractions. But it's the current pinnacle of human existence, so you have to do it at least once.

712. Check out Chicago.
☠ ☠ ☠

There's lots to do in the most frantic of Midwestern cities. But please, please, please, whatever you do, don't go there in winter (i.e., any months that aren't July or August).

713. Take in a show at Second City.
☠ ☠ ☠

A lot of very famous and talented people have come out of Second City over the years. There's a reason for that: Second City is really damned funny. Go and see. I recommend the e.t.c. stage.

I went there once, a long time ago, and got to shake the hand of Tim Meadows as he was walking out, after he did a hilarious show. The mainstage is in Chicago, but you can also catch a show in Toronto, Las Vegas, Detroit, Los Angeles, or Denver. Visit *www.secondcity.com*.

❐ 714. Break into a secure facility.
☠ ☠ ☠

The easiest way to do this is to walk right in, during business hours, pretending like you belong there. Carry a clipboard, and before someone notices you and walks up to ask what the hell you're doing, walk up to them and tell them to take you wherever it is you want to go. Oh, this is probably a federal offense.

❐ 715. Cross any red line painted on the ground of a property owned by the Department of Defense.
☠ ☠ ☠ ☠ ☠

Here's the deal: that red line is the demarcation between areas where you are—nominally—allowed to traverse freely, and those where you are most certainly not allowed to move about. Military people do not take kindly to people who are "breaking red." It's not a good thing to do. They will let you know this. Most often, they will let you know this while you are facedown on the pavement, with the barrel of a firearm pressed behind your ear, and a knee in the small of your back. That's if they don't decide to shoot first, which is their prerogative.

❏ 716. Visit an active nuclear reactor.
☠ ☠

In actuality, nuclear reactors are extremely safe mechanisms; there's plenty of shielding and security and whatnot. It's the radioactive fuel that's the scary thing. But most of that is locked up pretty well, and they're fairly careful with it. So go check it out. Tell me about it when you get back.

❏ 717. Explore a geographic area undiscovered or rarely visited by any other human beings.
☠ ☠ ☠ ☠ ☠

The real tough part is finding a place like that left on our planet. Once there, be really careful, because you don't quite know what is fatal to humans, yet.

NATURE THINGS

Our species has gone to great lengths to distance ourselves from nature. With cause: nature is a nasty, ugly thing, where living creatures die quite readily, in a variety of ways. So one great source of Things is the sensation of being present for a demonstration of one of nature's bitchier habits. Inland, you've got tornadoes and earthquakes. On the coasts, you've got typhoons/hurricanes and tidal waves. Everywhere, you've got mudslides, sinkholes, huge hail, lightning, and temperatures that fluctuate rapidly enough to freeze or fry a human.

Take your raincoat.

718. Look into an active volcano.

☠ ☠ ☠

There are over a thousand volcanoes on this planet. Go find one and check it out—tell the rest of us what it's like, will ya?

719. Outrun a lava flow.

☠ ☠ ☠ ☠ ☠

According to official government sources, lava can travel at speeds greater than 30 kilometers per hour, if channeled and moving downhill. Before unraveling the real mystery here, realize that you can't reasonably move that fast for any length of time. Of course, there are different kinds of lava, some more viscous than others. Not that you want to check the viscosity of the stuff before deciding whether or not to leave the area. Duh.

720. Flee a lahar.

☠ ☠ ☠ ☠ ☠

What's a lahar? You don't even want to know. It's a mixture of water and pieces of rock, flowing away from volcanoes, or in river valleys. Basically, this stuff takes on the consistency of wet cement and moves pretty darned fast—faster than lava, even. Lahars can also be hundreds of feet wide, and carry big honking boulders with them. You really don't ever want to see a lahar, yourself, with your own eyes.

721. Survive a tephra shower.

☠ ☠ ☠ ☠ – ☠ ☠ ☠ ☠ ☠,

depending on circumstances

You know how volcanoes can blow stuff up into the air? That

stuff is called tephra, and it includes both molten and solid rock. That stuff has to come down, too, via gravity. You don't really want to be under it, out in the open, when it does.

☐ 722. Experience an earthquake.

☠ – ☠ ☠ ☠ ☠ ☠, depending on conditions
When the very ground you're on starts to shake, accompanied by a significant rumbling, it's easy to leap to the conclusion that something just exploded, or that someone is dropping bombs on you. Even if you anticipated the natural occurrence, it is still extremely unsettling. Especially if you're trying to walk at the time.

☐ 723. Experience a tornado.

☠ – ☠ ☠ ☠ ☠ ☠, depending on conditions
Kids growing up in the Midwest get an education in an eerily Cold War–type survival technique: the duck-and-cover-'cause-a-tornado's-coming tactic. It's difficult to imagine that a force of nature will somehow be dissuaded from destroying you because you're cowering in a ditch or against a wall, but who knows? It might work. When you see the sky turn a dark, sickly green, and there's a creepy stillness amidst a summer storm, it's quite possible one of those brutal funnel clouds is about to touch down and wreak havoc. Best to avoid trailer parks in that situation.

☐ 724. Experience a hurricane.

☠ – ☠ ☠ ☠ ☠ ☠, depending on conditions
The tornado's coast-dwelling cousin, the hurricane can make the dirt-bound funnel seem tame in comparison. In addition to the horrific winds, you get the full benefit of nature at its most

malicious: deadly storms, floods, and huge waves inundating the area.

❏ 725. Experience an avalanche.

☠ – ☠ ☠ ☠ ☠ ☠, depending on conditions

Tons of ice, rock, and assorted debris falling at terminal velocity from elevation. It's going to stop when it wants to stop, and there's not a damned thing you can do about it (assuming, of course, we can anthropomorphize an inimical natural occurrence). This is probably best witnessed standing to the side or above the point at which the avalanche originates, as opposed to anywhere below. . . .

❏ 726. Experience a mudslide.

☠ – ☠ ☠ ☠ ☠ ☠, depending on conditions

The avalanche's junior partner, a mudslide can be just as deadly and destructive. Usually found in hilly areas where poor construction and land maintenance, combined with heavy rainfall, has led to serious erosion. If you think drowning is bad, try imagining drowning in mud.

❏ 727. Experience a sinkhole.

☠ – ☠ ☠ ☠ ☠ ☠, depending on conditions

Sort of a reverse-mudslide, the sinkhole can vary in speed and degree. Basically, the ground opens up to swallow anything on the surface; it can be a sudden implosion, or a gradual, creeping spread of the hole's perimeter, ceasing only when subterranean architecture is totally exposed. Not a fun place to be, for the most part.

728. Experience a tidal wave (tsunami).

☠ – ☠ ☠ ☠ ☠ ☠, depending on conditions

No, it's not something you want to try with your surfboard or water wings; this is a massive, crushing power, capable of obliterating just about anything along the coast, and can carry destruction well inland. If you can manage it, be airborne at the time.

729. Experience serious hail.

☠ – ☠ ☠ ☠ ☠ ☠, depending on conditions

As opposed to regular hail, which isn't quite as scary. Serious hail can come in three configurations: freakishly large hail, a dramatic amount of hail, or a combination of the two.

730. Experience a flood.

☠ – ☠ ☠ ☠ ☠ ☠, depending on conditions

Sudden inundation with water is a fear harbored by our species for thousands of years—with good reason. Anything from the urban peril of clogged runoff drains (the ominous "flash-flooding") to the rural deluge can wash away homes, vehicles, and certainly people. Be sure you know how to swim—that's just basic.

731. Experience lightning.

☠ – ☠ ☠ ☠ ☠ ☠, depending on conditions

Don't just sit on your front porch in the middle of July and gaze out comfortably at the beautiful display of heat lightning. Get out into some quasi-wilderness in the middle of a bitchin' storm and know what it's really like to see lightning nail something in dramatic fashion. Just hope it isn't you.

732. Let a really big, hairy spider walk across your body.

☠ ☠ ☠ – ☠ ☠ ☠ ☠ ☠,

depending on species

Pick any of the nasty (or nasty-looking) ones: a tarantula, a Sydney funnel-web, a Brazilian wanderer. . . . Feel those spiny hairs tickle your skin? See its globulous eye cluster, like the wet dream of a sci-fi special-effects designer? Everything in your body recoils at just the sight of it. So why are you touching it? Oh, and some of them are deadly.

733. Pet a porcupine.

☠ ☠

This is just like those little security blades in the driveways of some parking lots: If you drive over them in one direction, you're fine, but they'll slash your tires to pieces if you go the other way. A porcupine is nature's parking-lot-blade-thing. In one direction, you're okay; it's not soft or fluffy or anything—but in the other direction, well. . . .

734. Feed a wallaby.

☠ ☠

Yeah, they look just like cute miniature kangaroos, don't they? And, as we all know from a formative diet of Saturday-morning television programming, kangaroos are sweet, adorable, nice animals. So as you reach over the fence to offer a handful of Wallaby Kibble to a waiting marsupial, you will probably be quite shocked when it grabs the cuff of your sleeve, yanks you, jabs you a couple of times, and bites your palm. I know I was.

735. Milk a cow.
☠ ☠ ☠

Okay, if you've ever been to a dairy farm, then this isn't such a big deal. Of course, most of the modern American populace has never been to a dairy farm and don't realize that cows can step on people quite easily. Or kick them.

736. Harvest roe.
☠ ☠

We're talkin' caviar. Fish eggs, that is. That yummy, salty stuff that comes out of a fish's. . . . This is cold, slimy work. Thanks for doing it.

737. Get stung by a bee.
☠ – ☠ ☠ ☠ ☠ ☠, depending on circumstances
It's an annoying, painful sensation that can raise a welt and irritate you for hours. Unless, of course, you're one of those unlucky few who are horribly allergic to such afflictions—in which case, you might die. Bad.

738. Encounter a wolf.
☠ ☠ ☠ ☠

A family I knew in Colorado was specially licensed to keep wolves on their property. I was on their back patio one night, looking into the woods, with one of the family members with me. One second there was nothing there—the next, there were three pairs of red eyes staring at me, in a staggered line about twenty yards across. I was told to stay immobile, but the command wasn't really necessary: While something deep in the recesses of my brain was screaming, "Shouldn't be here. Shouldn't be here. Should be anywhere but here right now," my body was doing its best to shut down all ambulatory functions. The wolves approached to within about forty feet, and were joined by two others. There was something about them that was quite obviously not Dog. After a short while, I was told that it was all right to move inside the house again, which I did steadily, but without making any quick movements. Harrowing.

❑ 739. Look at the sun during an eclipse.

☠ ☠ – ?, depending on who you believe

Supposedly, this is bad for you. I am not quite sure how. Like, radiation, or something. Back in grade school, they made us build this weird cardboard eclipse-viewing thing, and warned us repeatedly not to look at the sun directly. They made it sound very, very bad, very dangerous. This was repeated to the point that it sounded so drastic that, if you failed to heed the warning, your eyes would melt and drip down your face, or your skull would explode, or your hair would catch on fire or something. So, of course, I did it. I currently retain 20/15 vision in both eyes. Maybe from looking at eclipses.

❑ 740. Experience hypoxia.

☠ ☠ ☠ ☠ ☠

Up at high altitudes, the air is rare—not much oxygen, the go-juice for human life. This can occur in high-flying aircraft, and the conditions can be simulated with a hyperbaric chamber. When the brain doesn't get enough oxygen, it does funny things. Your fine motor skills start to deteriorate, and your judgment follows.

Pretty soon, you're feeling drunk and goofy, and you seriously consider voting for whoever makes the best campaign promises. This can be deadly if you don't get some oxygen soon.

❐ 741. Experience nitrogen narcosis.

☠ ☠ ☠ ☠ ☠

If you're going to scuba, especially to any considerable depth (thirty meters or deeper), you should familiarize yourself with the risks and effects of this condition, as well as recognition of its symptoms. For some reason, nitrogen under high pressure (the main component of the air in your tanks) makes the human nervous system do some bizarre things: you can start to feel drunk, or elated, or extremely paranoid. Yes, it does sound like someone slipping you some bad drugs at a rave—but you're deep underwater, and the consequences of any irresponsible actions can be fatal.

❐ 742. Experience the "bends."

☠ ☠ ☠ ☠ ☠

The opposite cause of nitrogen narcosis: if you're scuba-diving, and come up too quickly, the compressed nitrogen which is usually absorbed by the body's tissues instead converts to tiny bubbles in the bloodstream. These get lodged in the tight corners, nooks, and crannies of the human body, which usually occur at the joints. Bad things can happen because of this, everything from skin rashes to sharp pains to death. This malady is not limited to divers; it can occur in anyone who moves rapidly from one environment to one with much less pressure, including people in pressurized mineshafts and those who fly in aircraft with unpressurized cabins.

☐ 743. Endure a brain concussion.

☠ ☠ – ☠ ☠ ☠ ☠ ☠,
depending on circumstances

The human brain doesn't quite fill the skull; it floats in a grue-some jelly bath, not quite touching the bone surrounding it. If you bonk your noggin violently against something, the brain sometimes strikes the side of the skull as the gooey suspension is forced out of the way (to be more accurate, the side of the skull is actually striking the brain, which is held motionless in the goop). This is almost never a good thing. Your brain is You, and you should refrain from bashing it as best you can.

☐ 744. Survive a venereal disease.

☠ ☠ ☠ – ☠ ☠ ☠ ☠ ☠,
depending on circumstances

Ahem. Yes. Well. In this, as in several other Things, the treat-ment can be somewhat worse than the malady.

☐ 745. Build a campfire.

☠ – ☠ ☠ ☠, depending on circumstances

Open flames are not only dangerous, but they're also fascinat-ing on a primordial level. Do your best to conduct this practice in a safe manner: have a source of fire-damping material (water, sand, etc.) nearby, know the wind direction and speed, and build it with sufficient firebreaks.

☐ 746. Build a campfire without using modern tools or accelerants.

☠ ☠ ☠ ☠

There are several methods for this: the ol' rubbing-sticks-together, flint and steel, etc. None of them is easy. Get in touch with your inner Neanderthal.

747. Engage in naked fire-jumping.

Those who have told me of this practice explain that there is a quasi-tribal cathartic thrill, probably a result of the instantaneous liberation from social conventions. I'm thinking beer was involved.

748. Throw a disposable lighter into a fire.

Once that fuel heats up, inside that little container, the flammable gas wants to force its way out of constraint, in any way possible. And once the shell melts or is cracked, all that fuel, usually in gaseous form, is going to detonate. Dramatically. Stand way, way back.

749. Throw live ammunition into a fire.

In counterintuitive fashion, the heated round is not going to "fire" as it would inside the chamber of a gun. Instead, the casing of the shell (usually heavier than the bullet itself) is going to launch backward, in an uncoordinated, unaimed manner. You still don't want to be anywhere near it, of course.

PART 1 PUBLIC THINGS

750. Run from a dog.

With the low center of gravity, four legs, and thousands of generations behind it, the dog is perfectly bred for chasing you. You, with your two spindly little legs and head bobbing way above the ground, are not designed to outrun anything. Try, anyway.

751. Intervene in a dogfight.

Not the brightest of ideas; a dog, in the midst of a battle, will flail about with its teeth and jaws, trying to bite pretty much anything. This means that even if you are trying to salvage your own pet, you are as likely to get bitten by it as by its opponent. Best to try some other method, such as hosing them both down with cold water, from a safe distance.

752. Kill the last remaining member of a species.

It might taste good.

753. Survive a disease.

– , depending on circumstances

Of all the big things that can smash you (rocks, gravity, vehicles, etc.), it's pretty amazing that few of them are as uniformly lethal as microbes, the tiny little buggers that can get inside your body and lay you out fast. Disease has killed far more people than any other cause, including warfare. Rest, and get plenty of fluids.

❏ 754. Survive a fever.

☠ ☠ – ☠ ☠ ☠ ☠ ☠,
depending on circumstances

Your body heats up, theoretically, to bake any nasties living inside of you. Of course, you aren't exactly designed to thrive at that temperature, either. On the plus side of the equation, fever dreams can be very vivid and interesting, and don't cost anything.

❏ 755. Become exposed to/ingest something you are allergic to.

☠ – ☠ ☠ ☠ ☠ ☠, depending on conditions

It's a spooky thing, to have a weakness that you have no control over whatsoever. No matter how you try to fight, or how tough you are, your body is going to react to this thing in an adverse way.

SUPERSTITIOUS THINGS

Sometimes, violating the precepts of a superstition/urban legend/old wives' tale is one of the most difficult things we can do; the social mores of the society we were raised in are a pretty stringent motivator, even if we know better. So just go ahead and try something you know to be rooted in a ridiculous, nonsensical belief; nothing bad is going to happen to you. Well, most likely.

❏ 756. Go outside (in the cold/rain/snow/winter) without a hat on.

☠

You probably won't catch a cold—a cold is a virus, and really doesn't care much about your head covering.

221

❏ **757. Go swimming less than a half-hour after a meal.**

☠ ☠

It's not clear why someone suggested that this practice be prohibited in the first place. . . . Something to do with muscle cramps, probably, but why would ingestion be linked to muscular performance? Of course, doing any sort of exercise on a full stomach can be a bit nauseating, and forceful vomiting while immersed in open water could be a little dangerous, so try to keep your food down.

❏ **758. Make that face.**

☠

Hold it. You know the one—the one that annoys the heck out of everyone, the one that you were told would freeze on your features permanently if you kept making it. Yeah, right. Facial muscles don't just randomly lock up—which is a good thing, considering the expressions we wear during orgasm.

❏ **759. Stay overnight in a house/cave/room/ building said to be "haunted."**

☠

That place in Amityville. Alcatraz. The Bunnyman Bridge in Virginia.

❏ **760. Start your own religion.**

☠ ☠ ☠ ☠

Most of the world's religions claim to say much the same thing as the others—they all lie. They all say something incredibly distinct, and they all want you to pay homage to their archaic methods and concepts. So be an individual, flaunt tradition, and become a heretic. Proselytize.

❐ 761. Debunk an urban legend.

You've got that friend/family member/dipshit coworker/acquaintance—you know the one. The one who keeps forwarding you stupid crap they've received via e-mail. Go surf over to *www .snopes.com* and find the page outlining how this particular stupidity is ridiculous. Copy and paste the link, and send it back. If he or she was churlish enough to include every recipient's e-mail address, use Reply to All, and let everyone know how goofy the sender is. Hopefully, a little public humiliation will quell the e-mailer's desire to continue the practice.

❐ 762. Refuse to forward a chain letter.

Go so far as to write back to the initiator (or at least the clown who passed it to you), deriding the sender for his or her misplaced belief in inane crap.

❐ 763. Refuse to put butter on a burn.

It seems almost certain that every person on the planet has that relative/friend/acquaintance who adamantly states that butter is the perfect salve for a burn wound. Butter, among its many nonmedicinal properties, contains a high amount of salt—and we all know how good salt is on an open wound. But hey, maybe your burned flesh tastes better with butter.

764. Swallow your gum.

Sure, someone once said that it messes with your digestive system. Whatever. Go ahead and swallow it, just to show them.

765. Put fresh flowers/plants in your hospital room.

There's an old wives' tale that suggests that fresh-cut foliage sucks oxygen out of a room. Which is just stupid: obviously, greenery sucks out carbon dioxide and exudes oxygen. Plus, flowers in your room make it look as if people really like you.

766. Survive a curse.

The power of the human mind is amazing—for instance, if you actually believe you are going to die, and you're physically infirm to begin with, it's quite possible you'll talk yourself into being a corpse. So let someone curse you, then make it a daily practice to call the curser on the telephone and announce the fact that you're still quite alive.

767. Throw a hat on a bed.

In some superstitious circles, this will result in something bad happening to you. Unless you have lice, what ill effect might spring from this cause?

❑ 768. Walk under a ladder.

☠ ☠

Who knows how refraining from this became superstition instead of simply remaining "a good way to avoid being bonked on the noggin by stuff dropped by whoever's on the ladder." But whatever—it's your Thing.

❑ 769. Step on a crack.

☠

Nobody's spine will suffer the slightest damage, I assure you.

❑ 770. Shower during a thunderstorm.

☠

Common knowledge has it that any stray lightning bolt that connects with your domicile while you are in the shower will course through your plumbing and use your body to complete the circuit, frying you like so much chicken. Common knowledge, of course, is largely comprised of stupidity spouted by morons. Go ahead and get clean, no matter what the weather is like.

❑ 771. Use a homemade contraceptive device or method.

☠ ☠ ☠ ☠ ☠

I had a friend who once tried to convince me that his utilization of plastic cling wrap was a great idea. I tried, momentarily, to disabuse him of his misplaced pride in innovation. It didn't work. I think his girlfriend ended up preggers. Boy, was I surprised.

PART

2

private
things

Some things are exciting, yet not for the prying eyes of others. And there are some Things that just can't involve others, for a variety of reasons (including good taste and nowhere to comfortably place your elbows). So go ahead and take the plunge—but keep 'em to yourself.

MISCELLANEOUS THINGS

There are those Things that don't fit neatly into other categories. This makes them no less fun or challenging, however. Take a look and see what you might like.

☐ 772. Feed a live animal to a snake.

☠ ☠

Sure, a snake will eat pithed food—I've even known people who kept snake treats in the freezer. But that's plainly unnatural, and unfair to the snake. The snake wants something fresh, like it was evolved to eat. And there are few things as fascinating as watching that timeless death-dance.

☐ 773. Blow something up with explosives.

☠ ☠ ☠ ☠

Explosives are nasty, despicable things. This is because, unlike projectile weapons, they are utterly indiscriminate. Oh, sure, there are nifty adaptations like shaped charges, but explosives really just comply with one set of rules: high school physics. Spooky. A gun, you can point. Explosives? Just be out of the way. Way out of the way.

☐ 774. Use military-grade explosive equipment.
☠ ☠ ☠

Oddly enough, this is probably the safest form of explosive available, because it was specifically designed to be used by even the humblest of junior-ranked enlisted personnel. A Claymore mine, for instance, has the helpful "This Side Toward Enemy" stamped on it, and a LAW rocket is emblazoned with a nifty cartoon explaining the procedure for arming and firing the device.

☐ 775. Use dynamite.
☠ ☠ ☠ ☠ ☠

This practice has a lot more to do with the fuse and the blasting cap than with the explosive itself. Still, it seems awful risky. Be very careful.

☐ 776. Use nitro.
☠ ☠ ☠ ☠ ☠ +

There's a good reason Nobel decided to use some sawdust to stabilize this explosive into dynamite: It's very tricky to work with, and entirely unforgiving.

☐ 777. Undertake a hands-on project (automotive repair, plumbing, carpentry, metalworking, computer networking, etc.) involving a field you know nothing about, have no training in, harbor no inclinations for, and generally dislike.
☠ ☠ ☠

Do the best job you can.

❐ 778. Build a house.

☠ ☠ ☠ ☠ ☠

Pretty much the ultimate in the Handiwork Department. If you can put together a human dwelling, you're certainly ahead of most of the global population.

❐ 779. Build a house you intend to live in yourself.

☠ ☠ ☠ ☠ ☠

There's the true test of your belief in your work. A poorly constructed domicile can kill you in so many, many ways.

❐ 780. Use a power tool.

☠ ☠ – ☠ ☠ ☠ ☠ ☠, depending on conditions

The tool doesn't care what it's working on. Be it concrete, wood, dirt, metal, glass, or human flesh, the tool will keep on doing whatever it's designed to do, unless it's switched off or loses power. Keep that in mind.

❐ 781. Use a lathe.

☠ ☠ – ☠ ☠ ☠ ☠ ☠, depending on conditions

This thing will spin your industrial medium continually, letting you cut and shape it into whatever shape you want (assuming that shape can be created with a series of grooves of different sizes and depths). It will also throw off debris at a furious pace, often like shrapnel, and even the thing itself, if you misapply force and break it.

❏ 782. Use a concussive nail-driver.

☠ ☠ ☠ ☠

This is basically a gun that fires nails instead of bullets, BBs, or other projectiles. You even load it with gunpowder cartridges. Bear in mind what that means in terms of the force of the nail flying out of the end, and what that could mean if you trigger it inadvertently.

❏ 783. Use an industrial-grade laser.

☠ ☠ ☠ ☠ ☠

In addition to the possibilities of slicing off or otherwise puncturing parts of your body, there's the omnipresent chance of instant blindness.

❏ 784. Spend a winter in Wisconsin.

☠ ☠ ☠

Yeah, that stinging feeling in your eyes? It's your tears starting to freeze in their ducts. Snowfall here is a lot different than in any non-Midwestern state. In Texas, those wimps shut everything down if there's two inches on the roads. In Wisconsin, if six feet fall overnight, McDonald's might close, but those school buses are running.

❏ 785. Spend a summer in Mississippi.

☠ ☠ ☠

There are a lot of unfair stereotypes made about Mississippi, about the people there, about the social mores, about the weather. Most of it is deserved. Some of the best food you'll ever eat, though. Wash it down with cold beer and try not to sweat too much.

❏ 786. Adopt a pet from an animal shelter.
☠ ☠ ☠ ☠

This is far more dangerous than buying a used car; true, with a used car, you're getting somebody else's problems, just like a used animal. But the worst thing a car will do is kill you, which really is over pretty quickly. You might fall in love with your used pet, and then realize too late (but too soon after you let it into your heart) that you'll have to put it to sleep because it's got some fatal, evil disease, and then you're worse off than before—now you've got a big pet-shaped hole in your life, and no pet.

Train . . .
❏ 787. . . . a dog.
☠

Dogs are pretty willing to be trained, and are well-suited for it. Thousands of years of peaceful cohabitation with humans has made them the ideal species for interaction and beneficial mutual coexistence. Do it the right way—without ever raising a hand to the animal—and you will reap great rewards in terms of obedience, loyalty, and exceptional behavior.

❏ 788. . . . a puppy.
☠ ☠

A little more involved than training an older dog. A puppy, while quite willing to follow your commands, is instinctually driven to do things that you would most likely not want it to do.

789. . . . a cat.

☠ ☠

Cats, unlike their canine counterparts, are not designed to take commands from humans, or perform repetitious behaviors not already ingrained in them through instinct and genetics. Doesn't mean you can't try, though. Funniest thing in the world is a cat on a leash. . . . Well, not the cat, per se, but the person holding the leash.

790. . . . a big cat.

☠ ☠ ☠ ☠ ☠

We're talking about predators here. Lions, tigers, cougars, lynx—heck, you can even take credit for training an ocelot. These are not playthings, and they aren't domesticated: They may be tame, but that's it. Even then, they have a base set of instinctual responses that include a variety of behaviors that may place you in danger, with little or no warning, in reaction to stimuli you might never know about. I once stood right outside the bars of a cage, alone, as a trainer opened the door, got inside, and let a fifteen-foot tiger jump on him. Scared the crap out of me, and I was safely beyond the bars.

791. . . . a rat.

☠ ☠

Clever little buggers, no question. I had a buddy who took a college science class for which he had to train a rat to perform a series of complicated maneuvers, start to finish, with no reward until the end. He trained it to run a James Bond course; dressed in a bow tie, the rat would sneak up on a plastic soldier, knock it

233

over, get in a toy car, "drive" the car to a certain point, get out, climb a wall, go paw-over-paw across a line suspended well above the ground, all in succession.

❐ 792. . . . a wild horse.
☠ ☠ ☠

This practice is also known as "breaking," which is a massive misnomer. The animal ends up trained, ready to accept people working alongside or atop it, instead of physically or mentally broken. A broken horse doesn't do anybody any good. A trained horse, however, is a prized possession. This takes an enormous amount of concentration, patience, diligence, and care.

❐ 793. . . . a bird.
☠ ☠ ☠ ☠

Take your choice of type: raptors (such as hunting falcons or hawks), mynas (imitative passerines), or babblers (talking parrots, cockatiels, etc.). No matter the type, birds are skittish, smelly, snapping animals, not prone to taking instruction readily. Sure, some might be as smart as five year-old children—but think about how tough it is to train a five-year-old.

❐ 794. Steal something.
☠ ☠ ☠ ☠

I swiped a corncob pipe (retail price: thirty-five cents) from Swan's Pharmacy when I was six years old. My face felt hot enough to use as a pants press, and my tiny prepubescent body exuded more sweat than it had in my entire life up until that point. What a rush. And I still feel guilty to this day.

☐ 795. Steal something of great value.
💀 💀 💀 💀

The jewels of an heiress. A foreign sports car. A vast amount of wealth in an incredibly liquid form, such as paper currency. Gold. It's called grand larceny, and it makes for good movies—but can you pull it off? Probably not.

☐ 796. Steal a car.
💀 💀 💀 💀 💀

In the old days, taking someone's primary form of transportation was called "rustling," and it was punishable by death. With good reason, too—our transport is a great part of who we are, what we do, and how we live. Now we call it "grand theft auto," and it should be punishable by death. Sometimes it is, too.

☐ 797. Hotwire a car.
💀 💀 💀

This is a really cool skill to have, just in case, you know, you misplace your car keys and don't have a Triple-A membership. Of course, with modern vehicles, this is an incredibly complex and difficult achievement. Might as well go get a degree in electronic engineering.

PART 2 PRIVATE THINGS

❐ 798. Run with scissors.
☠ ☠ ☠ ☠

Why do you think that every parent/teacher/grownup in the world told you not to do this all those years?

❐ 799. Reformat your hard drive.
☠ ☠ ☠ ☠

You've got information you've been saving for years. Aunt Eustace's address. The lifetime warranty number for your brake pads. All those URLs in your Favorites folder. Precious stuff, indeed. So back it up, carefully, and wipe your machine to start from scratch. Good luck.

❐ 800. Pick a lock.
☠

Locks, oddly, aren't as hard to defeat as you might imagine; they just take a little bit of time and perseverance, combined with a modicum of manual dexterity. Pick one of your own locks, as attempting this on someone else's may result in a rather long jail stint.

❐ 801. Try a wildly harebrained treatment for a fatal disease.
☠ ☠ ☠ ☠

Can't possibly hurt to try. Beats the alternative.

❐ 802. Mix household cleaners.
☠ ☠ ☠ ☠ ☠

There are infinite ways to combine, collect, and coagulate all sorts of nifty chemicals, using stuff you buy off the shelf at the

236

supermarket or hardware store. They can give you some funky results, too, like napalm, mustard gas, or chemical explosives. Much fun can ensue (if you don't kill yourself). You won't find any formulas in this book: There are other books (and the Internet) for that. Kids, don't try this at home. Or anywhere else you might get caught.

❏ 803. Take a cold shower.
☠ ☠ ☠

For some reason, this has entered our cultural consciousness as a deterrent to prurient urges. I don't know if it really works (never did for me), but it's all sorts of uncomfortable, there's no denying that.

❏ 804. Betray someone's trust.
☠ ☠ ☠ ☠

There are few things more embarrassing or irreplaceable as violated trust. Beware the consequences.

❏ 805. Look down the barrel of a loaded gun.
☠ ☠ ☠ ☠ ☠

There are few things more shock-dumb terrifying. If it ever happens, you may find yourself suddenly focused entirely on that single point in space, or you may find your mind wandering to other, totally unrelated ambient occurrences, such as what the air happens to smell like at the moment. Not a comforting sensation.

❐ **806. Look down the barrel of your own loaded gun.**

☠ ☠ ☠ ☠ ☠

I made the mistake, one time, of coming home from work early and surprising a roommate who had been wakened by a noise and knew where I kept a pistol. There's a moment I will always remember . . . and a new lesson: call first before entering anyone's living space. I think that's a worthwhile lesson.

❐ **807. Play Russian roulette.**

☠ ☠ ☠ ☠ ☠ +

Pick a multichambered weapon; a revolver is traditional. Insert one piece of ammunition into a single chamber. Close the cylinder. Spin it. Put barrel of gun to head, business-side of the gun against your temple. Pull trigger. There is just about nothing more crazy-dangerous than this form of suicide.

Put your fist through . . .
❐ **808. . . . a wall.**

☠ ☠ ☠

It's one of those childish displays of angry immaturity, striking out vindictively, trying to punish only yourself and an inanimate object. Feel better?

❐ **809. . . . a window.**

☠ ☠ ☠ ☠

Not only will this most likely hurt your fist, but you have to contend with the shards of glass that remain in the pane, perfectly positioned to slice through skin, flesh, and all those wonderful tendons, veins, and arteries beautifully exposed on your wrist and arm.

RELATIONSHIP THINGS

Love is the source of the most irrational behavior. Therefore, monkeying with it may be the most foolhardy thing you can do.

☐ **810. Act civilly toward someone whose opinions and viewpoints you find utterly reprehensible.**

☠ ☠

Most of us do this in some manner, anyway, without ever taking it as a dare. We accommodate someone out of politeness or fear or some other base urge—like telling that very hot person you are trying to get into bed that you agree that Pol Pot's musical genius was overshadowed by his political career.

☐ **811. Tell someone close to you that you find their opinions and viewpoints utterly reprehensible.**

☠ ☠ ☠ ☠

You want the fastest way to ensure that something will always be haunting your relationship, hanging over it like an evil miasma, something known but unsaid for the rest of the duration of time you know each other? Try this.

☐ 812. Flirt.
☠ ☠

Check out that cutie over there. Throw a wink, a nod. Smile at the person serving you food, and chat them up a little. Start something. Get a phone number or e-mail address. This is, of course, all sorts of troubling, for a variety of reasons. You could enrage a devoted significant other/admirer of the target of your flirtation, and they could choose to do you bodily harm. Likewise, maybe you only intended to be nice and friendly, and the recipient took it as a true romantic overture, and will now be hurt when you explain the misunderstanding. Dangerous fun.

☐ 813. Flirt with someone you're not attracted to, just because flirting is fun.
☠ ☠

Nothing really wrong with this, unless the other person becomes attracted to you and is expecting more than you're willing to put out. Let them know you're not really interested as soon as you recognize this situation.

☐ 814. Flirt with someone whose significant other is present.
☠ ☠ ☠

Okay. Okay. The only way to be cool and do this is when there are two couples present, and everyone's a friend of everyone else, and they all understand you're just joking. So do it that way. Anything else, and you're just a jerk.

1001 THINGS TO DO IF YOU DARE

240

☐ 815. Flirt with a foreigner while on vacation.
☠ ☠

Ummm . . . what other reason is there to travel the world?

☐ 816. Flirt with someone for the express purpose of getting something you want.
☠ ☠ ☠

Some people find this inappropriate. Maybe they're bad flirters. Or unattractive. Or both.

☐ 817. Befriend a professional dominatrix.
☠ ☠

They're people, too. They have problems with the rent, with relationships, with finding the right grocery store for all their shopping needs. They also just happen to be involved with stuff at work that might just disturb you. You don't want to hear about their day at the office.

☐ 818. Befriend a madam.
☠ ☠ ☠

You really wouldn't think it, but that sweet little old lady who is the go-between for hookers and johns might really be a sweet little old lady. She's there to make sure everyone's happy and that the party doesn't get out of hand. She also goes home at night.

☐ 819. Befriend a prostitute.
☠ ☠ ☠ ☠ ☠

Impossible.

PART 2 PRIVATE THINGS

820. Give your significant other general power of attorney.

☠ ☠ ☠ ☠ ☠

Marriage? Cliché. Diamonds? Useless, overpriced rocks, product of a perfect marketing/con job perpetrated by an oligarchy. This is the sure way to find out whether or not that other person is truly in love with you, or whether he or she is just wheedling to find a way to screw you royally. It can also be the express train to Doomed City. Enjoy the trip.

821. Ask your partner for a prenup.

☠ ☠ ☠ ☠

Want to really test the durability of your relationship? Asking for a three-way is passé. Having an affair is trite, and miniscule in comparison. Go ahead and ask your love-buddy to put their assertions of undying love and fealty down on paper. Be prepared to duck.

822. Get divorced.

☠ ☠ ☠ ☠ ☠ +

Look, make it easier on yourself: Drink a bunch of drain cleaner, stick a large magnum handgun in your mouth, then slip a plastic bag over your head and tie it off with a nylon noose. There's no reason to even mess around with this one—pure suicide. Did you know some people do this more than once? They never survive, though.

DATING THINGS

The ancient mating ritual. The human courter approaches the target tangentially, as if careless of the need for affection, pretending to be blasé—the target acts in the same manner. Somehow, they're supposed to end up in bed. Weird.

□ **823. Make a pass at an incredibly attractive stranger.**

☠ ☠ ☠ ☠

The funny thing is that the oft-touted anticliché is not true: Really attractive people do not intimidate most other people, and therefore go through their whole lives not being hit on. Nope. Instead, really attractive people are constantly hit on, often by people with far more to offer than you ever possibly could. Odds are almost certain that you will be shot down, and quite likely in a completely humiliating way. What have you got to lose but some self-respect? No guts, no glory.

□ **824. Tell someone you've had a crush on for a long time how you feel about her or him.**

☠ ☠

Just because it seems like every other book (or play, or movie, or TV program) suggests the opposite: This is a bad idea. "Bad" in the sense that you will never, ever have the relationship you once had with that person. Good, in the sense that you can stop wasting all that time being his or her emotional crutch and constant gainsaying suck-up, because the object of your desire is never going to deal with you anymore. Congrats for that.

☐ 825. Tell someone who has had a crush on you for a long time that you have no feelings for her or him.

☠

There's no easy way to do it. Rip off that adhesive bandage and be done with it. You should not have led her or him on all that time, anyway. Oh, and don't play innocent—you knew exactly what you were doing.

☐ 826. Tell a blind date you're only interested in the sex.

☠ ☠ ☠

There's something amazingly refreshing about the totally forthright, open, honest approach. Of course, you are guaranteed not to get laid. But it's still refreshing.

☐ 827. Tell a first date you're only interested in kinky sex.

☠ ☠ ☠ ☠ ☠

Know what? There are only so many people around who have complementary kinks. The odds of running across any of them by accident are pretty low, and, by a certain age, those with kinks have reluctantly come to this conclusion. So if you're on a first date, that means the other person already digs you to some extent anyway. Springing a kink on them will do two things: save you a lot of time waiting to get around to asking them once you've already established a relationship, and, on very rare occasions, pleasantly surprise the other person, who

just so happens to have that complementary kink. This works on a surprisingly frequent basis.

Date someone . . .

☐ **828. . . . far above your social station.**
☠ ☠

It can be a lot like one of those movies, plays, or books: That person's friends and family and colleagues may, in fact, resent you, and look down on you, and see you as just a scummy gold digger. That makes it kind of fun.

☐ **829. . . . far beneath your social station.**
☠

One really nice thing about this: You can always impress your date far more easily than if you were dealing with someone accustomed to your tax bracket.

☐ **830. . . . far better-looking than you.**
☠ ☠ ☠

From what I can gather, the difficulty of this is related to the people who will see the disparity of attractiveness between the two of you, and see that as an opportunity to make untoward advances on your partner. This can cause a lot of friction. Beware.

☐ **831. . . . far less attractive than you.**
☠ ☠ ☠

Not only will others wonder what you are doing with this partner, but your partner may become overly sensitive to his or her role in your relationship, to the point where jealousy and paranoia supersede affection and ardor.

❒ 832. . . . far above your intellectual level.
☠

Like with any other sport, you only get better at knowledgeable discourse and reasoned argument by playing above your skill level. It's a great form of mental exercise. Meanwhile, your partner's brain is atrophying.

❒ 833. . . . far beneath your intellectual level.
☠ ☠

There are only so many times you can explain what is happening in the movie before it becomes really, really irritating.

❒ 834. . . . of a different religious bent.
☠ ☠

It's cute right now. Think you're flouting convention, turning the world on its ear? Try talking about raising the kids. That'll be fun.

❒ 835. . . . of a different political bent.
☠ ☠ ☠ ☠

Doomed. Over and done before it began. You have to have some common ground besides sex. You just have to.

❒ 836. . . . of a different race.
☠

Not that big a deal, anymore. This is pretty straightforward, as long as the other aspects (religious notions, political persuasion, common background in terms of intellect, education, and finances) are all pretty much at parity.

☐ 837. . . . obviously deranged.
☠ ☠ ☠ ☠

None of us is normal. What you have to do is find one whose psychoses are tolerable to the point you can see living with it in the long term. But here's the dare: Try having a relationship of any duration with someone who is quite obviously whacked way out beyond the bell curve. Someone who talks to inanimate objects, or is convinced he or she is being observed by the government, or actually enjoys talk shows on television.

☐ 838. . . . ten (or more) years your junior.
☠ ☠

Oh, stop being so forgiving of yourself—you are exactly what everyone thinks you are, you scurvy little cradle-robber. Own up to it! Be proud of it! Every time you catch yourself describing your partner as "mature beyond his/her years," or anything to that effect, slap yourself in the face.

☐ 839. . . . ten (or more) years your senior.
☠ ☠

Yeah, they're just using you. Sometimes, it's fun to be used. And someone older usually knows a trick or two that will make them more appealing as a partner. Think of it as an extended, immersive research project.

PART 2 PRIVATE THINGS

247

840. Be stalked.

☠ ☠ ☠

There is nothing quite as flattering as having your very own stalker. Of course, there's nothing quite as spooky, either. It stops being fun real fast, so make the most of it while you can—before you're forced to call the authorities.

841. Stalk someone.

☠ ☠ ☠ ☠

No, it's not cool. No, it's not romantic. No, it's not sweet. It's ugly, and, depending on your jurisdiction, probably illegal.

842. Break up with someone.

☠– ☠ ☠ ☠ ☠, depending on circumstances

This can be incredibly painful, and far more devastating than many of the physical dangers posed by some of the Things in this book. More often, however, it's an awkward relief, one for which you might feel guilty. In that case, recognize it for what it is: a damned smart move—you should have gotten out earlier.

843. Perform a ridiculously romantic stunt, the kind of thing that would normally only be done by a fictional character, in the hopes of impressing a prospective partner.

☠ – ☠ ☠ ☠ ☠ ☠, depending on circumstances

Er—in reality, this usually only results in the target of your ardor being incredibly weirded-out by your mode of advance. Or with you in jail. This is why the behavior is mainly limited to fictional characters.

BEDROOM THINGS

Americans are prudes. More so than just about any other group in the history of the planet, American prudishness makes us hypocritical and nauseating. Which can add a nice zing to a Thing.

❏ 844. Take your significant other to a strip club.

☠ ☠

This can be quite uncomfortable. . . . It's sometimes tough to see the object of your affection drooling over someone else, right in front of you. But that's okay—it's sometimes tough for them, too. It is good to remember, though, that your partner is a sexual being, and has still chosen to hang out with you most of the time.

❏ 845. Tell your significant other what you were really thinking about while you two were having sex.

☠ ☠ ☠ ☠

See, this is where we often fail to communicate properly. There are certain things you should keep secret from your love interest—such as particular opinions regarding his or her extended family. But in the bedroom, the field should be wide open; honesty and forthright behavior can only favor you in the long run. This ain't easy—we're almost never that honest. Who knows? Maybe your sex toy was thinking the same thing you were. . . .

☐ 846. Have a one-night stand.

Yes, those tales of the torrid '70s have made their way down through the generations, to us, the people that were barely infants in the '70s. Supposedly, that mythic world offered promises of pandemic freaky sex, with an endless stream of willing partners, extremely low risk of pregnancy, and simple diseases that could be treated with a couple of hypodermic shots. This is now the type of dangerous activity akin to diving naked with sharks and an open wound.

☐ 847. Engage in oral sex.

Either giving or receiving. To be nice, do both.

☐ 848. Engage in anal sex.

Tomayto. Tomahto.

☐ 849. Try a three-way where both additional participants are of a gender you're attracted to.

This is the brass ring—the big one. The wildly bestest of them all. Be warned however: There may be a downside, especially if you're conducting this experiment with someone you care about. There is always the chance of jealousy complicating things. Moreover, this is reality, where the sights and sounds and tactile sensations involve actual people—so it won't feel like a porno, either during or after.

850. Try a three-way where only one participant is of a gender you're attracted to.

☠ ☠ ☠ ☠

This is a whole bunch different than the other configuration. It's a lot more likely—a lot more likely—the closest you'll get to the one that doesn't float your boat is a high-five at some point during the proceedings.

851. Try a four-way.

☠ ☠ ☠ ☠

And then continue to increase numerically for effect. You get the idea.

852. Sleep with a coworker.

☠ ☠ ☠ ☠

Everybody says how stupid and dangerous this is. Amazingly, they're actually correct. There is absolutely no good way to pull this off. You shouldn't try. Although, according to one recent survey, about half of Americans do.

853. Sleep with a superior.

☠ ☠ ☠

There's an amazing rush associated with this activity, as if you'd actually accomplished something. You haven't, of course.

854. Sleep with a subordinate.

☠ ☠ ☠ ☠

This is another one of those activities that seems like such a good idea at the time. Obviously, it's not, which is why there are so many company policies, sexual harassment laws, and mores aligned against it. You'd think that would make it more satisfying, too—but it doesn't. It's just sex. And, in this case, you—and you alone—are entirely responsible for the transgression. Oops.

☐ 855. Have sex in your workplace.
☠ ☠ ☠

Unless you're in the sex trade, this is definitely expressly forbidden. Also, conducting this activity will most likely involve at least one other Thing. Just about everybody thinks about this; we all think it will be fun and kooky. Remember, like most other adventurous sex, this is not taking place in your bedroom, and is bound to be more complicated and uncomfortable than in your fantasy.

☐ 856. Join the Mile-High Club.
☠ ☠ ☠

Yes. Sex in an aircraft at altitude. You are not the first to think of it. It's also probably a federal offense, depending on the attitude of the flight crew who catch you.

☐ 857. Have an affair with a married person.
☠ ☠ ☠

This is one of those clinically dumb activities usually enjoyed by younger people who don't know any better, or older people who don't care. It's also steeped in an unrealistic attraction of the forbidden. That wears off about the third time you have to go out a window with no pants.

❏ 858. Have sex in a moving vehicle.

☠ ☠ ☠

Not nearly as enjoyable or simple as you'd think—and, admit it, you've thought about it. In addition to the problems concerning space, privacy, and logistics, there is the hazard of traffic (pedestrian or otherwise).

❏ 859. Get yourself off in a roomful of people.

☠ ☠

For adolescents, chock to the gills with hormones and urges and such, this is pretty straightforward. A little more complicated for older folk.

❏ 860. Have sex in public.

☠ ☠

Usually, we like to have a bit of privacy in which to get on with our freak. Usually. Sometimes, though, having a bit of the thrill of being "caught" by others adds a little zing. Sometimes.

❏ 861. Visit a swingers' club.

☠ ☠

They're all there to scope you out, and you're there to scope them out. It's pretty much like a high school dance, only sleazier.

❏ 862. Visit an B/D/S/M (bondage/discipline/ sadism/masochism) club.

☠ ☠ ☠

The degree and extent to which human beings will go to get their jollies is fascinating, and not necessarily in a voyeuristic way (practitioners, sadly, don't often live up to your mental image of what they should look like). But from a sociological standpoint, it's wild.

❑ 863. Engage in mate-swapping.
☠ ☠ ☠ ☠

There's an entire American mythos surrounding this practice, steeped in mystique. Actually, it's a great way to ruin all sorts of relationships. Couples that can pull this off—and remain couples—are extremely rare.

❑ 864. Have unprotected sex with a stranger.
☠ ☠ ☠ ☠

There was a small window of opportunity, some time between the mid-seventies and mid-eighties, where this was not only feasible, but might only bring you the kind of harm that could be curtailed by a series of injections or a quick name-change. With the ugly introduction of HIV and DNA testing, the party ended quickly. Doing this today is a very dicey proposition, especially for women.

❑ 865. Have sex with an inanimate object.
☠ – ☠ ☠ ☠, depending on circumstances

Thousands of urban legends surround this practice. Maybe you can foment one. Good for you.

❏ 866. Have sex in the shower.
☠ ☠ ☠

Something about watery escapades makes them extremely torrid and exciting. If you don't deplete all the hot water, that is.
Nothing worse than cold water to, well, throw cold water on the
situation. Plus, anything watery has the additional detriment of
rinsing away lubrication. Tricky. You also need some balance. A
well-placed towel rack can make all the difference. Try not to
slip and die, as that would be very difficult for your partner to
explain.

❏ 867. Have sex in a bathtub.
☠ ☠ ☠

Not the most accommodating of surfaces, and tends to wear
quickly on elbows, knees, and any other bony protuberances.
And there's always the peril that water brings with it to the sex
act. So try to finish up quickly.

❏ 868. Have sex in a hot tub.
☠ ☠ ☠

Foamy, warm, splashy. With water jets. Seems like it would be
a lot of fun. Seems like it, doesn't it? Not as much fun as it
sounds.

❏ 869. Have sex in a swimming pool.
☠ ☠ ☠

Not just water, but cold, chlorinated water. Hmmmm . . . no.

PART 2 PRIVATE THINGS

❏ 870. Have a surreptitious affair.
☠ ☠ ☠ ☠

Er . . . so you're supposed to be in a monogamous arrangement . . . but there's this other person. . . . Well, what is the trite aphorism? "Illicit indulgences are really good in bed," or something? You're going to have to find out for yourself. And keep it on the down-low.

IDEOLOGICAL/PHILOSOPHICAL/ INTELLECTUAL THINGS

As adults, we're fairly convinced that our way of thinking is correct; it's gotten us this far, at least. We're pretty much set in our ways. Things that don't fit in our worldview, or things that contradict what we believe, are tossed away as useless or wrong. This series of Things might be the most difficult to choke down, then—these are things that might make you re-examine your perspective, or even change the way you think, which can be as uncomfortable as the incorrect underwear, until you get used to the new modes of thought.

❏ 871. Read a book. Start to finish. Cover to cover. Without skipping a single word, phrase, or jot of punctuation.
☠

You'd be surprised how many people haven't done this one. According to a study by the National Endowment for the Arts

(NEA), over 40 percent of Americans did not read a book in 2001, and the trend is downward. . . .

☐ 872. Read a book that you were supposed to read in high school or college, but found way too boring.
☠ ☠ ☠

Add to the challenge: make a solemn vow not to experience an orgasm until you've completed the work. Really make it difficult: pick something written by Proust, Dostoyevsky, or Dickens. Ultimate challenge: pick a ludicrously long book, like *Moby Dick* or *War and Peace*.

☐ 873. Read "Atlas Shrugged."
☠ ☠ ☠ ☠

Attempt to do so without having it change your worldview. Word of warning: the first seven-eighths are the easiest.

☐ 874. Find an intelligent person diametrically opposed to one of your most fundamental beliefs; carry on a rational, calm, logical conversation about that belief.
☠ ☠ ☠ ☠

Defend yourself and your belief only with sane argument. Nothing you believe is worth a damn unless you can coherently verbalize a cogent, objective thesis, supported by evidence and facts. No yelling.

❒ 875. **Find an intelligent person completely in tune with one of your most fundamental beliefs. Take the opposing view, and defend it as best you can.**
☠ ☠ ☠
Much more fun, as you get to challenge your own beliefs without having anything personally vested in the outcome.

❒ 876. **Take a course/class/seminar that forces you to re-examine your fundamental beliefs about who you are and what you want.**
☠ ☠
Every now and then, it's good to shake up your life by having a glance at the possible disparity between what you say you want, and what it is you really, actually want. Try to go in with an open mind. If nothing else, it may reinvigorate your interest in what you're already doing.

❒ 877. **Go get a college degree.**
☠ ☠ ☠
College is not about learning; it's about validating what it is you think and claim to know, and proving that you can demonstrate the patience and hardship of working toward a goal with seriously delayed gratification. So put up with those lousy professors, do the boring reading, and turn in your homework. You'll be pleased with yourself for doing so.

❏ 878. Go get a postgraduate degree.
☠ ☠ ☠ ☠

This one is more about actually knowing the topic. You're going to get more information than you can ever possibly absorb, so just stick it out and pay attention. Unlike your undergrad days, keep your books after the course is over; you'll never get anything near full value for 'em on the resale market, and they're valuable references.

❏ 879. Go get an industry certification.
☠ ☠ ☠

There are plenty of them out there; if you can think of the job, pastime, or habit, then someone, somewhere, is sure to offer a certification for it.

❏ 880. Get a certification for which you have no training, education, or skill whatsoever.
☠ ☠ ☠

It is possible, with a high degree of test-taking ability, some moxie, and a few choice references, to pull this off. Not quite sure what you'd do with it—although it seems like many people in many fields have taken this route.

❏ 881. Have the decency and guts to have a pet euthanized as a means of ending its misery.
☠ ☠ ☠

Some people say that the animal should be allowed to live as long as it possibly can, that animals don't feel pain the same way we do, and just being alive is enough for a pet. These people are assholes. If you don't agree with them, do the right thing.

☐ 882. Have the decency and guts to have a loved-one euthanized as a means of ending his or her misery.

☠ ☠ ☠ ☠ ☠

Do this, of course, only at that person's request. No matter what, you may face a murder rap, or media attention, so realize the onus before acting.

☐ 883. Solve a mystery.

☠ – ☠ ☠ ☠ ☠ ☠, depending on conditions

No, it doesn't have to be a murder, or even a fantastic crime or anything. Sometimes you can just do research to come up with an answer someone else overlooked, and discover the reason something occurred. Start small: Maybe you can find my missing car keys, for example.

☐ 884. Play a round of bingo with a host of people over the age of sixty.

☠ ☠

This is serious business. Don't play around, don't crack jokes—heck, don't even smile. They can smell weakness, and will denigrate and exploit it. And for the sake of your own feeble life, no matter what, do not call a false bingo.

❑ 885. Sit through someone else's religious service.

☠ ☠ ☠

Try to politely observe a different rite than the one with which you're comfortable, without being completely judgmental and patronizing. Find one dramatically disparate from your own. Endure it. Go ahead and be judgmental.

❑ 886. Sit through someone else's porn.

☠ ☠ ☠

Only slightly less disturbing than the preceding entry. Don't try this immediately following a meal.

❑ 887. Beg for money in a public setting while dressed in the full regalia of your religious/ ideological persuasion.

☠ ☠ ☠

Yes, all the rest of us look upon you with contempt and derision. But if you only get revenue from your fellow practitioners, then you're all just swapping coins, aren't you?

❑ 888. Accept—and meet—a deadline.

☠ – ☠ ☠ ☠, depending on circumstances

Labeling, measuring, and cataloging time is an artifice invented by humans. But now that we've decided to recognize temporal distinctions, you are in the position to decide if you're going to play along. If you accept a deadline for any kind of project or endeavor, folks are going to expect you to follow through. So do it—you said you would.

889. Learn a foreign language.
☠ ☠

You're probably pretty comfortable with your native tongue. It's something you understand, something you don't have to think about too much. Now try that all over again with another vocabulary and syntax. Want to be really daring? Try a language with an entirely different alphabet, like Russian or Korean.

890. Learn Spanish.
☠ ☠

For native English speakers, there are several facets of Spanish that will mess you up, including the reversed order of nouns and adjectives, words with loaded gender, and verb tenses that don't follow the standardized rules. Whatever else, though, it's much easier for English speakers to learn Spanish than the other way 'round.

891. Learn Italian.
☠ ☠

There are those (language experts, mostly) who claim that Spanish and Italian are totally separate languages. Or are they really the same language, and Italians and Spanish speakers are purposefully trying to confuse the rest of us? Whatever is true, try to nail down either language, and see for yourself.

892. Learn German.

☠ ☠

Basically, you get to curse at whomever you're talking to in German, no matter what it is you're saying. It's a guttural, harsh language, well suited to Germanic peoples.

893. Learn Russian.

☠ ☠ ☠

Oh, the Romance languages were too easy for you? Needed a bit of challenge? Well, welcome to the Cyrillic alphabet, bucko—more than a daunting obstacle in and of itself. This is not a language for wimps.

894. Learn Arabic.

☠ ☠ ☠ ☠

Is that really writing, or a modern form of bizarre cuneiform?

895. Learn Japanese.

☠ ☠ ☠ ☠

Sure, even a whole new alphabet didn't frighten you off—no big deal, you say. So how's about trying something that's painted rather than written, up and down, instead of side to side?

896. Learn Chinese.

☠ ☠ ☠ ☠

Next to English, this is the single human language with the most words. It's probably also the second most-complicated, in its variety of uses and rules and exceptions to those uses and rules. Good luck.

❏ 897. Invent your own language.
☠ ☠

It's been tried, and it's failed consistently. Language is messy, difficult, and full of exceptions to each inane rule. For some reason, a new, ordered, precise language has never supplanted any of the naturally occurring ones. Except among fourteen-year-old girls, who seem to have a genetic knack for this. Ben Franklin tried it, and it never caught on—what makes you think you can pull it off?

❏ 898. Learn a dead language.
☠ ☠ ☠ ☠

Not much call for 'em nowadays. 'Cause, you know—they're dead. Hence the name.

❏ 899. Learn Latin.
☠ ☠ ☠ ☠

Okay, I guess this is useful for pharmacists, doctors, priests, lawyers, and crossword puzzle freaks, but for normal people, it's just not going to come into play that often.

❏ 900. Learn an artificial language.
☠ ☠

Esperanto's a good one, for those who are into that kind of thing. They even made a movie with it, starring William Shatner.

❏ 901. Learn a purely visual language.

☠ ☠

Pick your favorite: American Sign Language, maritime signal flags, semaphore, etc., etc. Think of what a hit you'll be at parties.

❏ 902. Learn a purely auditory language.

☠ ☠ ☠

Morse or tap code. Back in the old days, you could have learned telephonic chimes for phone phreaking, but that's outmoded now.

❏ 903. Learn a purely tactile language.

☠ ☠ ☠ ☠

We're talking Braille. And a whole lot of patience.

❏ 904. Learn a computer language.

☠ ☠ ☠ ☠

There are plenty to choose from: BASIC, Cobol, C++, and the list goes on. Here's the big risk: After going through all that trouble to learn to communicate effectively with computers, you are in serious jeopardy of being outmoded rather quickly; the industry can switch to a newer language at the drop of the hat, and you're instantly obsolete. It's a big game of employment musical chairs, and you don't want to be the last one standing.

❏ 905. Learn higher math.

☠

It's a tricky set of rules, but once your brain is trained to think logically and objectively, it's not as hard as you might initially believe.

PART 2 PRIVATE THINGS

❏ 906. Learn calculus.

💀 💀

Again, with some practice and perseverance, this isn't as challenging as one might think.

❏ 907. Learn advanced calculus.

💀 💀 💀 💀 💀

"Imaginary numbers"? Enough said.

❏ 908. Update to a new technology, even after you've spent your entire life with an archaic form, and are totally unprepared for the change.

💀 💀 💀

This is an element of modern life, and will continue even more rapidly in the coming years. You're going to have to push yourself outside your comfort level, or risk being left behind financially and socially. Yes, it's time to lose the typewriter, Hoss. Ask a fourteen-year-old to help you.

❏ 909. Maintain use of an obsolete technology.

💀 💀

The world has passed you by, and the utility of the thing is decreasing every day. But you're comfortable with it, and it works for you, so why bother changing to something newer? That new thing is going to be obsolete in eighteen months, and you're going to have relearn how to use the next technology, anyway.

❏ 910. Haze a freshman.

There's a time-honored tradition of making those new entrants into the realm of higher education perform some amazingly goofy and humiliating acts. Not that we should stand on tradition and call that sufficient reason; instead, look at the freshman itself: a pathetic, smarmy, beggared organism, created solely for the abuse. So call it performing nature's bidding.

❏ 911. Stick to a personal conviction, even in the face of overwhelming public disapproval.

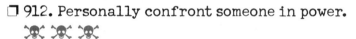

It's real easy to be sure and right and true when you're surrounded by a mob of gainsayers involved in some serious group-think. Now go and try it among the competition, adversaries, or enemy. Say what you mean, and don't back down.

❏ 912. Personally confront someone in power.

Teacher, politician, cop, employer, judge, parent—it doesn't matter. Stand up to them, challenge their authority, tell them when they're wrong. But make damned sure you're correct before you do it.

PLEASURE/PAIN THINGS

Our bodies are amazing—they are linked to our minds in a countless number of ways, and truly influence our perception of reality. The greatest motivators, really, are our sense of pain and pleasure. Exploit them—make them work for you. See what they can really do.

913. Pick the thing you are most afraid of; confront it.

☠ ☠ ☠ ☠

We've all got phobias—those things that make you cringe, even though you know there's no possible way the thing you're afraid of could possibly harm you (or harm you to the extent you fear it, anyway). Pick the big one, the whopper of them all, and go and do something along those lines that will push you beyond your toleration level of heebie-jeebies.

914. Visit a strip club.

☠ ☠ ☠

Taunt the strippers. They aren't looking at you; you don't exist for them. You are a wallet with legs. It is therefore their job to do everything necessary to get as much out of you as possible, within the rules. And the rules allow them to be callous, obnoxious, cruel, and downright evil. Return the favor. But remember—they have bouncers, and you don't.

915. Visit a brothel.

☠ ☠

The single most honest sexual encounter you will ever have. Not necessarily the most "pleasurable," just honest.

916. Visit a brothel in Amsterdam.

☠ ☠ ☠

Sure, they've got those famous windows in the Red Light District, but that's just for shopping, in my opinion. Those venues are cramped, far from luxurious, and there's always the notion

1001 THINGS TO DO IF YOU DARE

that the damned window isn't too far away. The brothels, on the other hand, are well-appointed and plush.

☐ 917. Visit a brothel in the United States.
☠ ☠

Basically, you've got to get to Nevada, where you'll quickly learn that while the places are decent, and the purveyors are very pleasant, it's not the glamour you expected. Also, supposedly, there are illicit brothels in every fair-sized American city, town, or burg. These are much more difficult to find, and the quality often diminishes with the legitimacy.

☐ 918. Visit a brothel in Australia.
☠ ☠ ☠

Good golly gumdrops. It really can't get much better than this. I mean, they like our accents. How is that possible?

☐ 919. Visit a brothel in South America.
☠ ☠ ☠

Any language barrier, of course, is easily surmounted by hard currency. No big surprise there.

☐ 920. Set fire to something you once held dear.
☠

Immolation is a time-honored means of converting a tangible thing to memory only. You can do this with just about anything (assuming it's not alive), and the practice has that poetic flair, with the bonus of catharsis. Do not do this if you are in a wheat field, petroleum refinery, or drought-ridden national forest.

□ 921. Undergo an invasive surgical procedure involving full anesthesia.

☠ ☠

There is nothing quite like coming up out of the narcoticized blur. . . . It's not like waking up at all. Instead, you're suddenly just Somewhere Else than you were a moment ago, but now you've got a sore throat and some additional pain in the part of your body where they just cut you open.

□ 922. Undergo an invasive surgical procedure involving local anesthesia.

☠ ☠ ☠

Watch the proceedings. There is no activity as surreal as seeing someone, who you've paid, mutilate your body right in front of you . . . and you can't feel a thing. The absolute worst possible configuration? Smelling your own flesh burning, watching it melt, and having all the sensation of a block of wood.

□ 923. Undergo an invasive surgical procedure involving no anesthesia.

☠ ☠ ☠ ☠

This is an egregiously evil custom, which some parents—and those persons allergic to, or otherwise hesitant about, anesthesia—elect for certain patients. Your brain is not equipped to deal with this form of barbarism and will rail against what is taking place. As well it should.

924. Have a root canal.
☠ ☠ ☠ ☠

You think you know pain? Real pain? Pain that makes you want to shrivel up and overdose on an opioid? Nope—not if you've never had a root canal, you don't know pain. An infected nerve in your jaw, maybe with a little abscess—now that's pain.

925. Walk on hot coals.
☠

This is not really daring at all; it's just a simple demonstration of certain physical principles, such as, "Gee whillickers, if I don't stand on the coals, they might not have enough time to burn me."

926. Crack your joints.
☠

Warning! All current necromancy, witch-doctory, and voodoo is quite clear on this point: Cracking your knuckles will lead to arthritis, rheumatism, jaundice, rubella, sleeping sickness, the vapors, and a host of other stuff that can't be cured. But it feels so good.

927. Experience suddenly becoming unconscious.
☠ ☠ ☠ ☠

It's almost cliché to drown and then be resuscitated—but that's really the best (if "best" can be used in this context) way to accomplish this one. Much better than blunt-force trauma, anyway. And still a little better than asphyxiation by choking. All in all, it's probably good to bear in mind that all possible methods leading to unconsciousness (besides sleeping, of course) run respective risks of brain damage.

☐ 928. Go through a nervous breakdown.

☠ ☠ ☠ ☠

Hey, this is your breakdown—you can let it take whatever form you desire. Some people just curl up into a little ball on the floor and gently sob until someone comes to take them to the hospital. Other people go full-blown bonkers, jump up on the furniture, and yell hysterically. Make the most of it; people are very forgiving when someone "suffers a nervous breakdown," much more forgiving than when dealing with someone who's just an asshole on a regular basis. Exploit that forgiveness and have some fun with your mental deterioration.

☐ 929. Endure a sweat lodge.

☠ ☠ – ☠ ☠ ☠ ☠, depending on conditions

This is a bit more than your basic sauna. Usually a hut made of natural materials, with a hole dug in the middle, where heated rocks are placed, and continually refreshed, to keep the temperature high and the interior atmosphere stifling. The longer the duration you can remain inside, the more daring.

☐ 930. Perform an activity that's good for you, without fail, every day for a month.

☠ ☠ ☠

Doesn't matter what it is: exercise, eating fruit, whatever. Make sure it's something you don't ordinarily do. The tricky part about this one isn't that you'll feel so transformed that the activity will become habit, and you'll do it forever after, and you will be a better person for it—oh, no. No, the tricky part is how dull and boring it will become by the second week, and how every fiber in your being will create excuses for you to stop. This is not easy.

☐ 931. Perform an activity that's bad for you, without fail, every day for a month.

Yeah, this one is a lot more likely to become habit than the good thing. Remember, it only counts if it's something you wouldn't normally do anyway.

☐ 932. Get an electric shock.
☠ ☠ ☠ ☠
A big electric shock. There are many, many ways to do this. Many high school science teachers have one of those big Tesla-ball thingies, expressly designed to zap unwary students. Or the rural approach: pissing on an electric fence, the subject of much legend and conjecture. Or just lick your finger and stick it in an outlet (which may kill you). Feel how all your muscles contract and joints flex, powerfully, instantly simultaneously. . . .

☐ 933. For a really big electrical shock, get hit with an electrical stun gun.
☠ ☠ ☠
Police departments use them all the time, so they must be safe, right? Right. What would be really cool is if you were holding a chain of light bulbs at the time, and lit them up as you shut

PART 2 PRIVATE THINGS

down. If you've ever been diagnosed with a heart condition, this might not be for you.

☐ **934. Try to re-enact Ben Franklin's famous experiment with lightning.**
☠ ☠ ☠ ☠ ☠

It's quite apparent to most scholars that Franklin was grounded when he performed his feat, or he would have ended up a crispy critter. Several imitators who tried the stunt in the months following Franklin's performance wound up quite dead.

☐ **935. Remove one of your own teeth with no outside assistance.**
☠ ☠ ☠ ☠

There are many traditional comedic methods for conducting this operation; almost none of them work. And a dental injury is one of the most painful you could ever experience. Lots of luck.

☐ **936. Stay awake for forty-eight hours straight, in the privacy of your own home.**
☠ ☠

You wouldn't think so from this list, but the brain is a pretty powerful device. It can make you do and see and hear and feel all sorts of things. . . . If you push your brain hard enough, mess with it to the extent that it feels the need to taunt you into giving it something (like, say, a REM state), it will produce a startling series of sensations and imagery. Much like a David Lynch film.

937. Stay awake for forty-eight hours straight, in the wilderness.

☠️ ☠️ ☠️

The variety and intensity of sounds that occur naturally in the wilderness are astounding—and are bound to wig you out after you've gone a sufficient amount of time without sleep.

INGESTION THINGS

Your mouth, esophagus, and stomach are the gateways to your digestive system, and, from there, to your entire body. Let me remind you of an old aphorism from the computer-processing field: GIGO ("Garbage In, Garbage Out"). Makes sense, doesn't it?

938. Eat an ice cream cone as fast as you can.

☠️

You're crazy—you're out of control. Stop now, before you hurt someone—including yourself.

939. Eat something from a fast-food restaurant.

☠️

You know it's bad for you. You know it will do terrible damage to your kidneys, waistline, and sense of well-being. But, dammit, there's something so darned . . . comforting about greasy, toxin-laden fast food. What is it? Nobody knows. Probably the carbohydrates.

❏ 940. Eat something from a street vendor.

☠

Botulism. Salmonella. Dyspepsia. These are words created and disseminated by the evil adversaries of fun and good times. They know nothing of what is Right and Wonderful. A hot dog from a Chicago corner cart, in season, far and away exceeds the deliciousness of steak tartare at a fancy-schmancy restaurant. Some say a hot dog with a sporting event in front of it is the prime delicacy; they are also wrong.

❏ 941. Eat something from a street vendor in another country.

☠ ☠ ☠

This is dangerous. Not just because of the micronasties that could infect your delicate bod, but because your gut is used to certain things, has spent a lifetime eating those things, and if you dump something wholly unfamiliar into it, your gut will become confused and angry with you.

❏ 942. Eat something you find utterly disgusting.

☠ ☠ ☠

Yeah, that steak tartare I already mentioned? That might qualify. Protein's good for you.

❏ 943. Eat something still moving.

☠ ☠ ☠ ☠

For me, this was a tentacle off an octopus. My Korean hosts asked me if I liked sushi, and I assured them I did, and they asked if I liked calamari, and I emphatically agreed, and they pulled out some writhing tentacles. I really thought they were yanking my chain, but then they started eating. It was like chewing rubber, and swallowing took an incredible amount of willpower. I found out later that there's extra danger in this practice; it's said that the still-active suckers can adhere to the throat on the way down your gullet, and choke you from the inside. I'm not sure I believe this assertion, but I'm still fairly convinced my Korean friends were more interested in messing with my head than snacking.

❑ 944. Eat an insect. Or a bug—like a worm.
☠ ☠ ☠

Squeeze out the gooey dirt-by-product first. Try the big red ants; they have a lemony aftertaste. And, yes, covering them in chocolate is cheating.

❑ 945. Kill a mammal with your bare hands.
☠ ☠ ☠

I love animals. I really do. And big-eyed, furry animals seem to be the nadir of wonderfulness; people who abuse them should be tortured themselves. So when I was in survival school and was chosen to kill our bunny for dinner, this was not an experience I relished. Did you know rabbits can scream? Yes, they can.

❑ 946. Prepare a dead mammal for consumption, and eat it.
☠ ☠

Lots of people do this every day; this is how they prepare food. If you are civilized, this falls out of the realm of your experience. It's good to know you can do it, if necessary.

❏ **947. Eat raw flesh from an animal or innards from a fish.**

☠ ☠ ☠

That bunny I had to kill . . . well, evidently, in survival situations, you are forced to make use of every last bit of nutrition available. This includes some unlikely portions of the critter. Like the eyeball.

❏ **948. Enter an eating contest.**

☠ ☠ ☠

There are all kinds, from your standard county fair pie-eating competition, to the professional how-many-sticks-of-butter-can-you-put-away-in-three-minutes. Ergh. There's actually a circuit for this kind of thing, as the prizes are surprisingly valuable. Even more bizarre—it seems that body mass has nothing to do with consumption capacity, as some of the best performers are skinny folk. So you might want to try it, no matter who you are.

❏ **949. Drink alcohol.**

☠

Yeah, seems pretty straightforward, doesn't it? Most of us do this all the time. For those who haven't, it can be a pretty big dare. Let's just say that it's neither as good or bad as you were told.

950. Drink enough alcohol to get you drunk.
☠

Again, not all that complicated, one would think. The catch, of course, is that as you're drinking, and getting closer to drunk, your desire—and wherewithal—for remembering to stop drinking is impaired.

951. Drink enough alcohol to make you vomit.
☠

This is a teenaged pastime, for those who have yet to understand that this is really not a pleasurable experience. We should all experience it at least once in our lives so that we know the dangers involved.

952. Drink enough alcohol to make you pass out.
☠ ☠ ☠

More dangerous than you'd think from the treatment in popular media. If you get to this point, you've cranked a good dose of toxins into your bloodstream. High school or college is the last time you should ever do anything so foolhardy.

953. Try a keg stand.
☠

File under "Stupid College Tricks." Have some friends hold you, inverted, over a keg of beer. Place your mouth on the nozzle. Quaff as much as you possibly can. No, I don't understand it either.

❑ 954. Do a beer bong.

Also known colloquially as the "shotgun" technique, this involves gravity, pressure, and the mystic forces of idiocy that infest young people, particularly when it comes to ingesting large amounts of mood-altering consumables.

❑ 955. Endure a hangover, and never mention it to anyone.

You take the ride, you pay the price. We've been there. We know about it. You don't have to share the experience with us; we get no vicarious thrill from it whatsoever. Just shut up and be miserable on your own.

❑ 956. Smoke a cigarette.

This is the latest form of social leprosy. Nobody couth in our society smokes cigarettes anymore; it is verboten. That's probably part of the attraction.

❑ 957. Smoke a cigar.

Very overrated. The smell is nice, but the sheer repetitive tease is annoying; you don't inhale, so what the heck is that all about? And if you're drinking while smoking your cigar, be sure to have plenty of water chasers; those things will dehydrate you in no time.

❐ 958. Smoke a pipe.

No big challenge there: everyone loves a pipe. Even those who don't like the smell (and they are rare, indeed), dig the visual cue. There's the whole Sherlock Holmes/Atticus Finch thing. Keeping it lit, however, is the real trick. Good luck with that.

❐ 959. Smoke a hookah.

Also known as "shisha," the hookah is that big water pipe that looks like a Middle Eastern industrial-grade bong. The tobacco used in such things is often adulterated with some heavy flavoring, such as fruit or scent.

❐ 960. Ingest a substance currently prohibited by law in your own jurisdiction.

Rumor has it that the thrills offered by these things, and the feelings they give, are well worth sacrificing such things as safety, quality control, and self-respect. Hard to believe, insofar as the most interesting drugs are now mainly available from your doctor.

❐ 961. Try some cannabis.

That leafy weed seems to cause quite an uproar. On the one hand, you've got the potheads, who are trying to convince us all that hemp backpacks will somehow prevent the massive, imminent backpack shortage facing our country. On the other, uptight, narrow-minded goofs are trying to convince us that the demon growth will destroy humanity if we so much as touch it. In between sit the rest of us; most who have tried it, many who use it occasionally, and those who just want everybody else to shut up already. It's going to be legal (like in parts of Alaska, Holland, Canada, and California), there's no question; we'd just rather it happen sooner rather than later, so we can get on with our lives already.

❑ 962. Try some cocaine.
☠ ☠ ☠

The happening drug of the 1980s. This may explain the big hair and androgynous nonsense.

❑ 963. Try some crack.
☠ ☠ ☠ ☠

While coke may be dangerous and addictive and all that other stuff the antifun bogeymen claim it to be, there also seems to be a direct correlation between the quality of the drug you buy (and the price!), and its addictive properties. Cheap purchase = low quality = highly addictive. This stuff is the bargain-basement version of cocaine, and supposedly has all the properties that would go along with such a low price.

❑ 964. Try some heroin.
☠ ☠ ☠ ☠ ☠

Almost a punch line in itself now, this poppy-derived drug has been the scourge of human beings who prefer consciousness for millennia. For some reason, it stays in fashion among those who have too much time and money on their hands. They rarely have either for long. Baffling in its continued ubiquity.

❒ 965. Try some opium.

☠ ☠ ☠ ☠

Heroin's little sister, this calming inebriate seems to have the effect of just basically making the user into a human body with the brain of a comatose squirrel. In the big scheme of things, I guess the best you could say about this one is that we rarely hear stories about crazed opium fiends ransacking private homes for money to fuel their habit. Well, not in modern literature, anyway.

❒ 966. Try some morphine.

☠ ☠ ☠

Another opiate, this one sees much use as a medical painkiller, which is where I ran across it. It does the trick, no foolin'.

❒ 967. Try some psychoactive mushrooms.

☠ ☠

There are many, many varieties of these, with proponents lauding their favorites. It's a fungus. Which people eat or smoke to mess with their heads. And there you have it.

❒ 968. Try some LSD.

☠ ☠ ☠

A synthesized, concentrated form of the stuff you get from a particular mushroom mold, this drug is supposed to affect your mind in countless trippy ways.

969. Try some peyote.

☠ ☠ ☠ ☠

Some Native American tribes use this for religious purposes. It involves a fair amount of projectile vomiting. To each his own.

970. Try some amphetamines.

☠ ☠ ☠

Known as "speed," basically because it's supposed to keep you awake, active, and ready for action. How will you get your beauty sleep?

971. Try some methamphetamines.

☠ ☠ ☠ ☠

A refined form of amphetamines, and the genre of which "crystal meth," the current foundation for hysteria, is a member. All I know about this crap is that it couldn't possibly be as bad as everyone else makes it out to be, otherwise the free world would be facing a terror reminiscent of a drive-in zombie movie. And that I can't buy good cold remedies easily because of government overreaction to it.

972. Contravene the direct orders of a prescription pharmaceutical.

☠ ☠ ☠

So this one time, I had an appointment to go be interviewed by a police psychologist (long story). I was taking some rather serious knock-you-on-your-ass painkillers for a tooth infection, and the instructions clearly stated that I shouldn't even consider

driving a motor vehicle. I told the detective who had scheduled the appointment, but she said to go anyway. So I did. The shrink never seemed to notice. This did little to bolster my flagging belief in the entire "science" of psychoanalysis.

☐ 973. Mix pharmaceuticals with alcohol, even when advised otherwise.
☠ ☠
Not as big a deal as it's made out to be.

☐ 974. Try an inhalant.
☠ ☠ ☠ ☠
Also known as "fun with household goods." You can huff just about anything with fumes, to greater or lesser effect. Gasoline, paint, paint thinner, and the traditional favorite, model airplane glue—the list goes on and on. All you need is a bag (paper or plastic), a fume-filled substance, and an express desire to cause irreparable loss of brain cells.

☐ 975. Become addicted to something; try to give it up cold turkey.
☠ ☠ ☠
Pick your poison: sugar, caffeine, nicotine. Get good and comfortable with it—let it become not just a joy, not just a habit, but a true need. Put it away for a good length of time. Say, a week. Or a month. Hold out on yourself just for giggles. Resume in that welcoming, self-immolating junkie manner.

❏ **976. Add a significant percentage to your own body weight.**

☠ ☠

Maybe you have to bulk up for a competitive sport, or you have just conquered some malady and want to regain your former appearance. You'd be surprised how difficult this is for some people. Try a lot of bad food and torpor.

❏ **977. Lose a significant percentage of your own body weight.**

☠ ☠ ☠

You have that piece of Goal Clothing—maybe it's a pair of pants, or a swimsuit, or a business suit—or it could be that you just don't want to look terrible when summer rolls around. Or you're involved in a sporting event where you have to make a certain weight cutoff. Diet and exercise. Only way to go.

❏ **978. Make your own beer.**

☠

There are those snobs who suggest that homebrew far surpasses any store-bought concoction. They often add all sorts of bizarre flavorings, such as fruit and other edibles.

❏ **979. Make your own wine.**

☠ ☠

Do you have any idea how many damned grapes you have to crush to make a single bottle of wine? About eight bunches— that's around 390 grapes! And there are about 10,000 things that can go wrong as you're trying to vint the stuff. A cheap bottle off the shelf will cost you a lot less than your sanity.

☐ 980. Make your own hard liquor.
☠ ☠ ☠

While quite illegal in most places, this is an American tradition dating waaaaayyyy back to one of the first uses of official federal troops: the Whiskey Rebellion. Of course, another American tradition is to go blind from drinking bathtub gin.

☐ 981. Make your own narcotics.
☠ ☠ ☠ ☠ ☠

From what I can gather, this involves some high school chemistry skills, a desire to make money, and a lot of cold-and-flu remedies. Not only is this activity wickedly illegal, but it's also extremely prone to exploding everything and everyone associated with it.

☐ 982. Bake a cake.
☠

Not nearly as easy as you might think. There are plenty of ways to screw it up, and only one way to get it right.

☐ 983. Make a soufflé.
☠ ☠

Oh, you did everything correctly. You got all the ingredients, mixed them properly, in the right order. You've got the oven set at the right temperature, for the proper duration. But that sucker still fell, didn't it?

984. Eat an inanimate object.

☠ ☠

Ever see those actors in spy movies eat the secret message? Go ahead and give it a whirl. It used to be fashionable to eat glass, too—at least among circus freaks.

985. Eat in a revolving restaurant.

☠

Someone thought it was a good idea to combine the thrills of a merry-go-round and the pleasures of fine dining. That person may have been a six-year-old. Usually, these things are at the tops of tall buildings, so that you can view a full panorama of the locale.

986. Drink the national drink in as many countries as possible.

☠ ☠ ☠

Soju in Korea. Aguardiente in Colombia. Sake in Japan. Vodka in Russia. You may note a thread here: It would seem, from these examples, that the national drinks of most countries are oily, violent, clear liquids, intended to either inebriate the drinker or cauterize wounds. This is not necessarily true: Many national drinks are oily, violent, tinted liquids.

987. Steal honey from wild bees.

☠ ☠ ☠

Yes, it's true: The bees don't care for this practice. And they will make you aware of it in the way that bees have of showing their displeasure. Repeatedly.

988. Raise honeybees.
☠ ☠ ☠

For the honey, of course. Not, I mean, so that you have an entire colony of vicious little creatures who will do your bidding at your whim. Because they won't—bees aren't docile enough to become evil hench-creatures. Darn.

989. Raise honeybees in an area infested with Africanized bees.
☠ ☠ ☠ ☠

My neighbor Jeremy, who has about fifty colonies around town, says the Africanized variety "aren't as bad as people make 'em out to be." Still, it ain't easy raising a crop of the gold stuff with that type around. "You have to re-queen every year," he explains. Plus, he says, the imported strain of bees "sting a lot more." Yeah, "re-queening" and "sting a lot more" sounds like quite a decent Thing to me; good for you, if you decide to try.

990. Purify your own potable water.
☠ – ☠ ☠ ☠, depending on circumstances

There are a host of ways to do this, including everything from distilling with heat or evaporation, to iodine tablets, to high-tech filtration systems. Obviously, the more time- and labor-intensive, the more daring. And you have nobody but yourself to blame if you get poisoned.

991. Experience the effects of a riot control chemical agent.

☠ ☠ ☠

You've got your CS, CN, and CR gases, and your capsicum-based pepper sprays. All of them are collectively and colloquially known as "tear gas," and all of them make you want to expel every bit of snot from your body as rapidly as possible. Just a whiff is enough to get the idea—suffering the full effects of long-term exposure isn't necessary or advised.

992. Go spicy.

☠ – ☠ ☠ ☠, depending on conditions

Many sources claim to have "the world's spiciest [whatever]." I'm always wary of anyone who makes a statement involving exclusivity and/or extremity without qualifiers. Still, if you and your intestinal tract are up to it, try to out-spice your palate without causing any second-degree burns. Wasabi, habanero and other chili peppers, horseradish, curry, garlic, ginger, mustard, and many more types of spices can be combined into a dish that can truly harm human beings. Make it as powerful as you can stand.

993. Take a soft fast.

☠ – ☠ ☠ ☠ ☠ ☠, depending on duration

Give up food for twenty-four hours. Longer, if you can manage it. You'd be surprised how quickly your mind gets past your stomach. Keep drinking lots and lots of water. I don't care what anybody says—starving yourself is a great way to lose weight. You just won't remain healthy while doing so.

994. Take a hard fast.

☠ ☠ ☠ – ☠ ☠ ☠ ☠ ☠,
depending on duration

Give up both food and water for at least twelve hours; ingest nothing during that time. This is not easy—your body is going to be really pissed at you. It's amazing how your entire existence will be clouded by thoughts of sustenance for the duration—aliens could come down from space, fire you from your job, rape the family pet, and trash your car, and you'd still be thinking, "Gee, if only I could have some water and a muffin, I could sort this all out."

995. Eat fresh seafood, right out of the water.

☠ ☠

Fresh veggies are good, of course. As is the flesh of wild game, caught in its natural habitat. But fresh seafood is an experience a cut above all else. Yum.

996. Prepare an artichoke for consumption by a human being.

☠ ☠

The artichoke is a formidable opponent to its own ingestion. It has been designed by evolution to ward off the most tenacious of attackers; it's equipped with sharp spines, stiff outer leaves, and a core layered in thistles. So you've got to handle it carefully, and cook it beyond resistance. Try steaming in a microwave.

❑ 997. Eat an artichoke.
☠ ☠ ☠

It doesn't seemed designed for edibility—and, in fact, downing one is a tricky exercise. You have to carefully scrape off the meaty pulp from the bottom-third of each leaf, using your teeth, while carefully guarding your lips from slices and punctures from the tip and edges. Then, when going for the heart, you have to extract the yummy stuff from its protective coat of bitter thistles, or wind up with a mouthful of nastiness. Well worth it, though.

❑ 998. Drink some coffee.
☠ ☠

In the past few years, there has been plenty of hubbub about the dangers of smoking tobacco, and how it probably leads to cancer. But there are plenty of people who never smoked a day in their life who have had the Big C; one theory has it that coffee is the agent. There's all sorts of poisons in there, not the least of which is caffeine, and one thing we know—if nothing else, it ain't good for you. Everyone seems to drink it; it seems more addictive than cigarettes. I've tried it a couple of times. . . . I'll stick to smoking.

❑ 999. Drink Turkish coffee.
☠ ☠ ☠

Might as well mainline the concoction by shooting it straight into an artery. This is not your grandmother's coffee—this is a no foolin', high-octane kick in the kidneys, and it will jazz you on several levels, both with the muddy caffeine and the treacly sweetener. Don't play with this.

1000. Drink Irish coffee.

Because uppers alone are not enough to entice you, add a downer to the mix; in this case, alcohol combined with the usual caffeine and sugar. Howdy.

1001. Drink some tea.

The choice of sophisticated palates, among caffeinated beverages. Really, the worst risk here is that you'll be accused of being British.

PART 2 PUBLIC THINGS

ABOUT THE AUTHOR

On a $20 bet, the author jumped out a second-story high school window when he was seventeen. He tore some cartilage in his left knee. Unfortunately, he did not learn from the financial disparity of this experience and has since done a bunch of silly things. He's flown a glider and a Cessna; rappelled down a cliff face and out of a hovering helicopter; driven a race car; dumped a motorcycle; nearly drowned while trying to learn to surf (ditto water-skiing); went scuba-diving off the Great Barrier Reef; slalomed double black diamond runs in the Rocky Mountains; rafted class IV rapids and canoed Class III; gone the distance in numerous boxing matches and other martial arts events (and lost just as many times); run with a herd of bulls at the request of his crazed editor; fired the combined small-arms inventory of both NATO and the former Warsaw Pact; visited brothels on five continents; eaten a variety of bizarre things (including rattlesnake, horseflesh, and something that was still moving); supplied security services to the FBI, Department of Defense, and Department of Homeland Security; worked as an undercover investigative journalist; served as a military officer on classified counterdrug operations; and maintained a long-term relationship with a redhead.

He admits he might be stupid.